THE
CHARISMATIC
LEADER

To the grandchildren—
Ellie, Mitch, Amy, Matthew, and Kaylee

THE
CHARISMATIC
LEADER

THE PRESENTATION OF SELF AND THE CREATION OF EDUCATIONAL SETTINGS

DALE L. BRUBAKER

CORWIN PRESS
A SAGE Publications Company
Thousand Oaks, California

For information:

Corwin Press
A Sage Publications Company
2455 Teller Road
Thousand Oaks, California 91320
www.corwinpress.com

Sage Publications Ltd.
1 Oliver's Yard
55 City Road
London EC1Y 1SP
United Kingdom

Sage Publications India Pvt. Ltd.
B-42, Panchsheel Enclave
Post Box 4109
New Delhi 110 017 India

Printed in the United States of America

Library of Congress Cataloging-in-Publication Data

Brubaker, Dale L.
The charismatic leader : the presentation of self and the creation of educational settings / Dale L. Brubaker.
    p. cm.
Includes bibliographical references and index.
ISBN 1-4129-1695-X (cloth)—ISBN 1-4129-1696-8 (pbk.)
    1. Educational leadership. 2. School management and organization.
3. Self-presentation. I. Title.
LB2806.B82 2006
371.2—dc22   2005003266

This book is printed on acid-free paper.

05   06   07   08   09   10   9   8   7   6   5   4   3   2   1

Acquisitions Editor:	Kylee Liegl
Editorial Assistant:	Jaime Cuvier
Production Editor:	Kristen Gibson
Copy Editor:	Kristin Bergstad
Typesetter:	C&M Digitals (P) Ltd.
Proofreader:	Penelope Sippel
Indexer:	Naomi Linzer
Cover Designer:	Rose Storey

Contents

Preface

This book, whose primary audience is teacher-leaders, assistant principals, principals, central office leaders, and superintendents of schools, focuses on three keys to successful educational leadership: (1) *Know thyself*, a foundation of understanding that helps one construct meaning from what has been experienced as well as a sense of what one is becoming; (2) *know how to present yourself well* in order to achieve personal and organizational goals and objectives; and (3) *know how to give leadership to the creation of educational settings*.

Earlier research we conducted on assistant principal, principal, and superintendent derailment revealed that problems with interpersonal relations were a key factor (Brubaker & Coble, 1997). Lack of communication and poor communication were frequently cited by respondents as examples of poor interpersonal skills. Incompetence, defined as the inability to carry out major role functions, was another leadership problem that led to derailment. Internal and external political conflict, difficulty in molding a staff, lack of follow-through, and overdependence on the board of education were other causes of administrator derailment.

Most of these problems were related to poor presentation-of-self skills and inadequate knowledge as to how to give leadership to the creation of educational settings. When we used the term *presentation of self*, we meant *performances*—defined as "all the activity of a given participant on a given occasion which serves to influence in any way any of the other participants" (Goffman, 1959, p. 15). In short, a major challenge facing educational leaders is to find ways to improve their own performances as well as the performances of those they lead—especially teachers. Performances, therefore, have both *a personal face* and *an organizational face.* This is to say that individuals and organizations may thrive or become derailed. Their relationship is symbiotic.

Educational leaders as professionals are able to articulate what they are doing and why. This articulation occurs in performances, and these performances take many forms: speaking, written communication (hard copy and electronic), nonverbal communication (body language and fronts), and listening.

Unfortunately, *teacher education programs,* usually centered in colleges and universities, provide few opportunities for prospective and present teachers to practice speaking to adults (Gordon, 2004; Sarason, 1999, 2004). It is this vacuum in teacher education that calls for special attention in professional development efforts. At the same time, the matters of written communication, nonverbal communication, and listening need to be emphasized more.

It is also true that *administrator education programs,* usually centered in colleges and universities, can provide more and richer opportunities to practice speaking to adults about what they are doing as professional educators and why (Gordon, 2004; Sarason, 2004). Written communication, nonverbal communication, and listening also need greater emphasis. (It is recognized that many teacher and administrator education programs are giving more attention to reflective thinking and writing than in the past. In previous years, too many programs overemphasized technical activities and skills.)

Two major figures who did research and writing on the presentation of self and the creation of educational settings deserve greater attention in teacher education and administrator education: Erving Goffman (1959), author of *The Presentation of Self in Everyday Life,* and Seymour B. Sarason (1972), author of *The Creation of Settings and the Future Societies.* These seminal works and the conceptual frameworks constructed by their authors are the springboard for the present book.

"The Prologue: A Cautionary Tale" takes us into a junior high school's "walk your child's schedule night," an open-house situation where a math teacher demonstrates his incompetence in a dramatic way. It raises the questions, "Why is it that presentation of self is such a problem for many educators?" "And, why is it that the junior high school math teacher's principal gave little, if any, attention to teachers' presentation of self problems?" More specifically, "Why didn't the principal create professional development settings that would give teachers an opportunity to improve their presentation of self?" The ninth-grade algebra teacher's poor presentation of self is a public relations problem, for it calls into question in a public forum his competence and by association the expertise of his colleagues as well as the school's administration. Perhaps even more important, the algebra teacher's inability to articulate a rationale for his instruction in relation to his colleagues' classes demonstrates a major communication problem within the school as a learning community. Teachers, administrators, and support staff have probably spent little time *talking* about their teaching practices and the reasons for such practices among themselves. We may also assume that without such talk there is little opportunity for adult educators to sharpen their *listening* skills on such matters. Furthermore, it calls into question whether adult educators in the school have engaged in *written communication* with each other, parents, and others that highlights best instructional practices and the rationale for such practices. In short, the cautionary tale demonstrates that a sense of *connection* is missing between the ninth-grade algebra teacher and the subject matter he uses as well as a connection with others involved in instruction and learning in the school community (Darling-Hammond, 1997).

Chapter 1, "The Civilities of Leadership: Attitudes, Behaviors, Tools, and Skills," focuses on civilities essential in order to present oneself well while creating educational settings. Seemingly small acts of kindness and acceptance of responsibilities can make a real difference in the culture of schools and school systems. It is also true that a major characteristic of civil leadership is willingness to stand up and be counted in influencing the governance of the school system as a whole and learning settings in the schools where leaders reside.

Chapter 2, "Teams, Teaming, and the Creation of Educational Settings," discusses ways in which working with others can help you avoid the twin enemies of loneliness and boredom. We tend to think of settings and communities in a geographical sense, but this chapter makes its clear that there are also communities of shared experience.

Chapter 3, "Professional Development on the Presentation of Self and the Creation of Educational Settings," describes teacher and administrator professional development ideas aimed at helping participants become more effective in presenting self and creating educational settings. The need for more attention to meeting this challenge is established, after which ways in which this need can be met are brought to the reader's attention. The question that will be addressed is, "Now that I am conscious of the importance of presentation of self and the creation of educational settings, what can I do as a professional development leader to apply my new understandings?"

Effective professional development doesn't simply spring from school culture. Effective professional development leadership creates an enriched school culture. And, "any significant attempt at school improvement will have a greater chance of success if it is integrated with effective professional development" (Gordon, 2004, p. 7).

The Charismatic Leader: The Presentation of Self and the Creation of Educational Settings emphasizes the idea that the leader you are becoming is what is really important. You are not a static, closed-system organism; you are instead in the process of experiencing possibilities that you have not yet even imagined. It is precisely this idea of becoming a better leader that is so exciting and challenging. This thesis fits with my definition of creative leadership as using your talents to help others identify and use their talents. The pleasure associated with these understandings grows when it is shared.

It is interesting to turn to any dictionary to discover the meaning of *charisma*. You will find that it is a gift that allows you to influence others. It is a kind of virtue associated with an assigned position, such as a teacher leader, an assistant principal, a principal, a central office administrator, or superintendent of schools. To use this gift wisely is an awesome responsibility and opportunity to make a difference in the lives of children, young adults, colleagues, parents, and others in the community. The purpose of this book is to help you as an educational leader to meet this challenge.

The Charismatic Leader: The Presentation of Self and the Creation of Educational Settings presents several snapshots—brief sketches—that illustrate key points in a personal way. The effect of these snapshots is to take you, the reader, backstage into the lives of educators as decision makers as they present themselves in creating educational settings.

You, the reader, will discover in reading this book that preservice and advanced education of teachers and administrators gives considerable attention to the matters of "What should I do?" and "How should I do it?" Methods for doing things have had a central place in teacher and administrator education since education's inception. They appeal to the pragmatic inclinations of teachers and administrators. However, effective presentation of self by educators must move beyond technical skills to the "Why?" question: "What is the rationale for the decisions I make and how can I clearly articulate my reasons for doing things when conversing with parents and others?" It is my belief that the successful integration of rationale and presentation-of-self skills depends on the educator's love of ideas. It is this passion for ideas and ways to implement them in educational settings that will make a real difference in reaching children, colleagues, parents, and others interested in improving our schools. When the passion of the leader meets the curiosity of others, learning takes root and action follows. It is at this point that persistence becomes important so that the core values of the leader and core group are sustained in the culture of the school and/or school system.

Finally, students, colleagues, and I have entered into spirited conversations in answering the question, "How much can an educator improve his or her presentation of self?" If you are shy, can you become an extrovert? If your strength is in presenting broad conceptual ideas rather than details to an audience, can you become a detail expert, or vice versa? If you are basically a person who blends in, can you become an outgoing leader? Goffman (1959) answers this question by saying that the cornerstone of presentation of self must be authenticity or genuineness. To try to become the opposite of your basic personality or inner self is to become a performance risk as the audience will quickly recognize you as a phony (Brubaker & Coble, 2005). Some politicians and television personalities have tried to change their basic personalities with the result being that the audience joins the performer in giving more attention to the way the self is presented than to the message being conveyed. The thesis of the present book is that you as an effective leader will learn to present yourself: "Know thyself" and "To thine own self be true." The first proverb is from Socrates and the second proverb is Polonius' advice to his son Laertes in Shakespeare's *Hamlet*. The marriage of knowing self and being true to self makes it possible for both the leader and the audience to recognize that courage is "the most precious asset anyone can bring to the public arena" (Califano, 2004, p. 491). Courage is the bedrock of two other characteristics necessary for success in the public arena: determining the right course of action and having "the tenacity to stay the course" (Califano, 2004, p. 492). School and school-system leaders who exercise these characteristics are civil servants, citizens, who demonstrate civility and leadership.

What, then, can you learn about presentation of self while not changing your basic personality? Richard Amme (2003c), former television anchor and CEO of Rick Amme Associates, advises us to concentrate on skills such as "listening, message content, focus, strategy, tactics, doing and saying the right thing, preparation, rehearsal, collaboration, motivation, and team building" (p. 4). It is in participating in these professional development experiences that *nuances,* subtle experiences or variations, become *instinct,* patterns of activity that reflect one's inner self (Brubaker & Coble, 2005). When you achieve this state, you achieve a kind of presentation-of-self success that leads to the feeling of true community beneficial to others and yourself. You have met the challenge of doing something interesting for your audience *and* yourself.

You will note that appendices are included to help you personally as you read this book and also give leadership to others in professional development settings. For example, Appendix A provides you, the professional development leader, with a detailed outline or map to help those you lead improve their presentation of self. Other appendices are self-inventories relating to presentation-of-self attitudes and skills. References to appropriate appendices are in parentheses throughout the text. We found with our pilot program on the presentation of self and the creation of educational settings that the self-inventories gave each participant the opportunity to assess self, after which these assessments were useful in stimulating group discussion. The result was personal and group ownership of ideas learned.

In order to have a conversation about what happens to you in reading and applying ideas from this book, please e-mail me at <dlbrubak@uncg.edu>. I promise a response.

Acknowledgments

In reviewing the correspondence with persons associated with the publication of this work, it became clear that it takes a community to give birth to a book. The most important person in a publishing company, from the author's point of view, is the editor, who will serve as advocate, facilitator, and closer. Kylee Liegl, whose Northern Michigan roots I share, has used her own particular genius to initiate, coordinate, and complete each step of the publishing process for the last three books I have authored or coauthored. She combines the creativity of an artist with the precision of a wordsmith, for which I give thanks. Her editorial assistant, Jaime Cuvier, is on top of the details so essential in the editing process. She consistently gave me the support I needed to complete this book. I also want to thank Kristen Gibson, Production Editor, for the excellence she brings to her work. I always know when a manuscript reaches her that it is in good hands and the book will be completed with taste and elegance.

R. Murray Thomas, scholar and friend, gave me the first extensive critique of this writing project and helped me see that the original manuscript was three books rather than one. Other reviewers confirmed this critique, thus leading to a shorter but more focused book.

Seymour B. Sarason, scholar and friend, brought my attention to doing research and writing on the psychology of creating educational settings. His influence is apparent throughout this book.

Finally, doctoral students at the University of North Carolina, Greensboro, have served as a sounding board for the ideas in this book for more than three decades. They have supported my view that teaching, research, and writing can and should be integrated.

Corwin Press gratefully acknowledges the contributions of the following reviewers:

Dr. Frank Buck
Principal
Graham Elementary School
Talladega, AL

Dr. Karen L. Tichy
Associate Superintendent for Instruction
Catholic Education Office
Archdiocese of St. Louis, MO
St. Louis, MO

Susan Clark
Associate Professor
University of Akron
Akron, OH

About the Author

 Dale L. Brubaker is Professor of Educational Leadership and Cultural Studies at the University of North Carolina at Greensboro. He has also served on the faculties of the University of California, Santa Barbara, and the University of Wisconsin, Milwaukee. He received his PhD in Foundations of Education from Michigan State University. He is the author or coauthor of numerous books on education and educational leadership, including *Curriculum Planning: The Dynamics of Theory and Practice, Creative Survival in Educational Bureaucracies, Theses and Dissertations, Avoiding Thesis and Dissertation Pitfalls, The Teacher as Decision-Maker* (Corwin Press), *Staying on Track: An Educational Leader's Guide to Preventing Derailment and Ensuring Personal and Organizational Success* (Corwin Press), *Creative Curriculum Leadership: Inspiring and Empowering Your School Community* (Corwin Press), and *The Hidden Leader: Leadership Lessons on the Potential Within* (Corwin Press).

Prologue

A Cautionary Tale

It was a Tuesday night in October when my wife and I attended the open house at our son's junior high school. Parents were invited to walk the schedule of their child in order to meet teachers who would provide an overview and rationale for the classes they teach. A ten-minute presentation would be followed by a five-minute question-and-answer period. The whole process seemed to be fairly routine until we entered Mr. Jones's ninth-grade algebra class. His opening remarks were somewhat interesting, but it was the question-and-answer session that caught the attention of the 20 parents in attendance. A bright and articulate mother raised her hand and said, "Mr. Jones, how will this ninth-grade algebra class help my child when he is in high school and college?" It was the body language of the audience that demonstrated their personal interest in the question and its impending answer. They leaned forward and all eyes and ears awaited Mr. Jones's answer. "I have no earthly idea," Mr. Jones responded. A collective gasp followed, after which the parents filed out of the classroom.

Three things came to mind as I tried to make sense out of this experience. First, Mr. Jones missed an opportunity to connect his own instructional efforts with those of high school and college teachers. Second, Mr. Jones's poor performance had both a personal and an organizational face. He and his school suffered from his cryptic answer. Third, cause—indeed blame—for his sad showing, was not easy to assign. I did know, however, that Mr. Jones's *presentation of self* was wanting and the reasons for this were worthy of investigation.

My immediate hypothesis was that the junior high school principal, the officially designated leader of the school, was ultimately responsible for what went on in the school and a conversation with him might help me understand this situation better. Since I had an administrative intern in this junior high school, I was able to have several informal talks with the principal about professional development activities in general and parent involvement in particular. It was clear from these contacts that improving students' test scores was the be-all and end-all of staff development—a focus consistent with the school system's motto: STUDENT ACHIEVEMENT UP, COSTS DOWN.

The principal invited me to attend a teacher workshop during which an outside expert coached teachers to teach to the test by involving students in exercises and materials that would align instruction with test items. After the workshop, the principal took me aside and told me a story that demonstrated why he was retiring at the end of the year:

> Being a principal these days is like being in a hospital at night. They come into your room every two hours and say, "Are you doing okay?" They think they're making you better by checking on you. All I want and need is a good night's sleep.

Feeling that I had a good read on the culture of this junior high school and the principal's role in it, I decided to tell him what happened when we walked our son's schedule at open house and received a less-than-satisfactory answer from the algebra teacher. The principal wasn't surprised and said that he didn't know of any school system that had *presentation-of-self* activities for teachers as part of their staff development programs. He then added, "You need to talk to teacher education professors. After all, it is their responsibility to prepare teachers to talk to parents about what they are doing and why."

What the principal said made sense. If schools are consumed with staff development activities designed to raise test scores, then it seems reasonable that teacher education preservice programs should prepare teachers to talk to parents and others about what they are doing and why. I therefore interviewed a number of teacher educators at a nearby university in order to get a handle on whether or not *presentation of self* is emphasized in preservice education and, if so, in what ways.

I basically got the story that follows from preservice teacher educators:

> Most of our classes are quite large. We have the students think through and write lesson plans and units of study but we don't take the time to have students practice *speaking* in front of the class as if they were talking to parents and other adults. And, they certainly are not evaluated or tested on their ability to speak in front of adults.

I pointed out that a major hallmark of professionals is that they can explain to others what they are doing and why. Respondents agreed and said that the *writing* of lesson plans and the like afforded students the opportunity to do this.

Assured that preservice teacher education students have little opportunity for *oral* practice describing what they intend to do instructionally in their teacher education classes, I asked, "Are *presentation-of-self* skills emphasized as part of their student teaching experiences?" Respondents said, "What do you mean by presentation-of-self skills?" I answered by telling the story of my experience with the ninth-grade algebra teacher. One teacher educator's answer is a good summary of the responses I got from others:

> We don't give student teachers practice in orally responding to questions like the one asked of the ninth-grade algebra teacher. Student teachers may, however, observe how their mentors behave in such situations. And, we do give attention to the importance of the way teachers dress and

their use of good English. We also use cases to stimulate discussion of the moral dimensions of teaching as well as other key issues facing new teachers.

I left my interviews feeling that the story of the ninth-grade algebra teacher is indeed a cautionary tale—a warning that we need to systematically give attention to ways in which teachers and administrators can give attention to and improve presentation-of-self skills in one-on-one, small group, and large group settings. If we meet this challenge, parents, other adults, teachers, administrators, children, and indeed the whole school and school system culture will be richer for the effort.

Note: Please turn to Appendix M for seminar participants' list of the characteristics a teacher should have at an open house/walk-the-schedule night.

1

The Civilities of Leadership

Attitudes, Behaviors, Tools, and Skills

Civility is hardly the only way to live, but it is the only way that is worthwhile.

Peck (1993, p. 54)

Genuine civilities convey a sense of possibilities—"We can do it."

Anonymous

You are punished if you write to the authorities on behalf of another prisoner—say a sick man who is not getting any medical attention. The authorities say, "Look, your letters don't help." And they are logically right. But there exists another, inner logic: the prisoner who writes such a letter may not save his neighbor in the next cell, but he saves his soul.

Shcharansky (1986, p. 38)

Most of the behaviors discussed in this chapter are simple kindnesses or civilities that are not dramatic or even visible to many people. But at times it takes great courage to exercise one's civil rights as Anatoli Shcharansky describes in the third opening quote. In February 1986, Shcharansky—Soviet Jew, dissident, and accused American spy—was released from a Soviet prison to Israel, and freedom, after nine years in custody. His weight had varied from 81 to 165 pounds. He had become not only a powerful voice of dissent in the Soviet Union but also a bridge between Soviet Jewry and the rest of the human rights movement. Writing a letter on behalf of another person, an act of conviction and courage, can make a tremendous difference for the letter writer even if it doesn't bring about a change in the behavior of the oppressor. The Shcharansky quote sounds as if it could have been written by Mohandas Gandhi, Hindu religious leader and social reformer.

Occasionally we hear of an educational leader who rises above bureaucratic structure to stand up for a teacher, colleague, or student to take a stand on an important moral issue. A crusty veteran superintendent from the state of New York shared with me his views on this matter:

> If you aren't willing to go out on a limb for someone who has been treated unfairly, you don't have any right to have the position you have. In fact, this is the difference between a leader and a manager. A real leader is willing to risk doing what is right no matter what the consequences are.

When manners and civilities are invoked simply to get the approval of others, they are self-serving and as such usually don't have the ring of truth, authenticity, and integrity. When manners and politeness are used in this way, they communicate the leader's desire to avoid pain, and yet maintaining the health of a person or organization often involves a good deal of pain (Peck, 1993). To work through the pain in the interest of students and colleagues who are at risk is to use one's biases for a moral cause. William Buckley (1982) underscores how bias can be a kind of advantage in such situations: "Ken Galbraith and I have in common what strikes some as a disadvantage, but isn't: namely our plainspoken bias which gives a harnessing energy to our work" (p. 239). Buckley, a conservative, and Galbraith, a liberal, respect each other's commitments.

THE TABLE MANNERS OF LEADERSHIP

When I was a child I was asked to set the table before dinner. My immediate inclination was to resist the request, but I discovered with time that there was a sense of security and order in the task—something that gave me the feeling that I was making an important contribution to the dinner hour.

What I didn't realize at the time was that this "table manner" was one of several that set the stage for good conversation among family members. (How foreign this sounds to a generation that has learned to place dinner on a TV tray and head for the family room.) The dinner hour was a time to exchange ideas and opinions, a time to converse and listen. In short, it was a time to learn from each other—a time to sharpen thinking, speaking, and listening skills.

I recently asked a third-grade teacher what she had accomplished with her class this year. Her response was quite remarkable:

> One of the main things that I gave attention to this year was table manners in the cafeteria. Most of the students in my class had not learned the most elementary manners while eating—things like, how to hold their eating utensils, how to talk without yelling and how to listen to each other. I knew that if they didn't learn these things along the way that they would get in high school and not know how to behave in restaurants and other similar places. I found that once the students practiced these table manners that they actually found them both useful and enjoyable.

This teacher and my parents were beginning to develop what Roland Nelson, a former university president and leadership author, calls "the table manners of leadership" (Brubaker,

2004, p. 109). By this he means those small behaviors that facilitate an exchange of information and feelings that leads to learning and better relationships. Stated another way, the table manners of leadership are not used to manipulate people as objects within a bureaucratic hierarchy (Peck, 1993). Rather, they are used to create environments where persons can learn from each other in lateral relationships with each other. Table manners of leadership are skills and tools that let others know that you value your relationships with them—an attitude that others respect. The following snapshot, as with other snapshots throughout this book, takes you, the reader, to school and school-system locations in order to give you a backstage view of the author's ideas in action. These locations are the backdrop or context in which educational leaders make decisions on the firing line. The first snapshot illustrates the role of a secretary in creating a school culture that doesn't invite people into the school. The second snapshot illustrates how a secretary with good table manners of leadership invites persons into the school.

Snapshot 1.1   My First Encounter in an Elementary School

It was a beautiful spring day when I first experienced Raven Elementary School. I immediately noticed how well kept the school's grounds were. I could smell the wild onions from the first grass cutting of the year. And, there were beds of spring flowers just beginning to bloom. As I approached the main entrance I saw an attractive welcoming sign with its greeting in English and Spanish.

As I entered the main office, I saw a small group of adults, teachers and assistants, gathered around the secretary's desk. I stood there for several minutes watching the secretary sell clothes and beauty products (what I later learned was a side-business, with most of her products displayed in the teachers' lounge).

When the secretary approached me, there was no greeting of any kind, simply a quizzical "Yes?" I explained that I needed information on this particular magnet school and was surprised when she did not give me any written literature on Raven Elementary School. In fact, I was left with the feeling that the secretary didn't want her world interrupted. I also noticed that she had poor English: "The principal usually don't come in this early as she is out with the buses."

Snapshot 1.2   My Second Encounter in the School

My child didn't get into our first choice of magnet schools and so I returned once again to Raven Elementary School, a school with a math/science emphasis. The flowers I saw earlier in the spring were now in full bloom and the school grounds were immaculate.

I was surprised on entering the front office to be greeted by a newly hired secretary: "Good morning! Welcome to our school. I'm Miss Bradburn, the school secretary. How may I help you?" I explained that our child wanted to register as a student in the school. Miss Bradburn turned to her well-organized file cabinet, gave me some photocopied handouts, and told me what I needed to do in order to register our child. I immediately noticed Miss Bradburn's professionalism and good English—in contrast to that of the earlier secretary.

Miss Bradburn left me with the impression that she enjoyed her job, had pride in Raven Elementary School, and found my child and me to be special people deserving of attention.

Entrance and Exit Rituals

Entrance and exit rituals are important in any setting (see Appendix I for an entrance and exit ritual inventory). The preceding snapshots, or *scenes* in the language of Goffman (1959), vividly illustrate differences in two individuals' entrance ritual performances and the settings in which such performances took place. One of the adages in the luxury hotel business is that "if you manage the first and last impressions of a guest properly, then you'll have a happy guest" (Kleinfield, 1989, p. 36). Since both snapshots were located in the same school or physical setting, the school grounds were a real plus for they sent the message that administrators cared enough about this school and its occupants to have inviting lawns and flowers as well as a well-kept building exterior. Furthermore, the welcome sign in both English and Spanish demonstrated inclusion.

The secretary in the first snapshot had a conflict of interest or divided loyalty between her work at school and her private business. She *set the stage* for the visiting parent with mixed signals, thus conveying the message that the core values of the school itself were ambiguous. The immediate question that comes to mind is, "Why did the principal of Raven Elementary School allow this to happen?" (When bringing this snapshot to the attention of principals I have talked to in leadership seminars across the nation, the following is a summary of their reactions:

> Some school systems have policies that clearly state that school employees can't engage in such sales practices, others don't. The enforcement of such policies in schools that have them is often uneven and depends on the principal and those in central office who supervise the principal.

Unfortunately, the secretary, in part because of her divided interests, was not well organized and didn't have the printed information requested by the visitor. Her poor English was an inadvertent *misrepresentation* of educational professionalism. In conclusion, the secretary was what Goffman called a *performance risk.*

The second secretary used *dramatic realization* for her authentic performance, expressed during the interaction as what she wished to convey—a positive invitation to the school, its magnet program, and the educators in the school. By giving her timely, complete, and undivided attention to the visitor interested in this magnet school, Miss Bradburn exhibited special attention-giving behavior or what Goffman calls *audience segregation,* thus leaving the visitor with the feeling that he and his child were important—the ultimate compliment to any person. She showed the magnet program and school at its best, what Goffman called *idealization.*

It is worth noting with regard to entrance rituals that one of the first things hotel workers are told is that eye contact is a necessary behavior for greeting guests when they arrive at the hotel (Kleinfield, 1989). Such contact communicates your willingness to go out of your way to help persons entering the setting, and it says you are risking a certain kind of vulnerability on their behalf.

It has always been interesting to me to watch some leaders use smiles and other nonverbal behaviors to relax persons entering a setting. They also exhibit the ability to establish a connection with so-called small talk. Leaders who are sensitive to entrance rituals quickly read a situation and go the extra mile to help others. I recently had a very difficult, bad-weather flight from Atlanta to Boston. The clerk at the reception desk registered me in a bureaucratic, on-automatic-pilot way. I walked to a chair in the lobby, obviously shaken and tired from my difficult flight. An assistant manager of the hotel, who read my body language, asked me if she could get me coffee or a drink. I smiled and asked if she had any cranberry juice. She went to the kitchen and returned with a large bottle of cranberry juice. From my vantage point as a traveler who had faced bitter cold, snow, and a challenging flight, she seemed like an angel. Interestingly enough, one of the first things I did when returning home was to go to my notes from this trip, find her name and the address of the hotel, and write to the CEO of the hotel chain with a copy to the manager and assistant manager. She went the extra mile and deserved positive recognition for doing so.

Leaders who give attention to entrance rituals know the importance of the physical setting. For example, one school principal inherited a high counter that served as a barrier between guests and the secretary. The counter was removed to facilitate exchange of ideas and feelings. Another principal instructed secretaries and student assistants to begin conversations with guests by saying, "Welcome to *our* school. How may I help you?"

A good energy level on the part of the greeter is important, but it is not sufficient in itself. Guests want to know that school leaders have a sense of purpose so that children and adults will be involved in meaningful activity. A clear and concise vision statement communicates this sense of direction: "Everything we do here is aimed at helping children and adults become the best they can be." This general vision statement can be followed by more specific goals for the school. These statements are of little value if their owners can't share them with visitors in their conversations during normal school activity.

Goffman's use of the word *decorum* is helpful as we think of entrance rituals. The principal, secretary, receptionist, or teacher should know that visitors are influenced by the way in which school people comport themselves "while in visual or aural range . . . but not necessarily engaged in talk with them" (Goffman, 1959, p. 107). It is fascinating to simply sit in a chair in the school office and listen to the way in which adults relate to each other and the students. It is in such situations that the unobtrusive guest hears comments that reflect what Goffman calls *treatment of the absent.* Teachers and secretaries will make comments about colleagues and students who are not within earshot. High school student assistants' remarks are especially interesting when the outside observer is within aural range.

Exit rituals are as important as entrance rituals. (It is worth noting that many religious services have both a processional and recessional—the entrance of the choir and clerics and their exit.) A major purpose of the exit ritual is to leave the participants, especially visitors, with the feeling that what they have experienced is worthwhile. The principal and other educators in the school who walk parents and other guests to the door have the opportunity to prolong their conversation and demonstrate their care for the guests. It is an opportunity to summarize what has happened during the visit, thank visitors for their interest in the children and the school, and invite them back for another visit. It is during exit rituals that principals are reminded that "there is no more loyal guest than one who has a problem that gets fixed" (Kleinfield, 1989, p. 32). Luxury hotel surveys have also revealed time and again "that guests very much like being called by name" (Kleinfield, 1989, p. 35). A certain distanced respect is usually communicated with the use of Mr. and Ms. unless the host or hostess is on a first-name basis with the guest.

With regard to exit rituals, it is also important to remember that the way you, the leader, leave is often the way you will be remembered (Woodward, 1999). I recently heard two speeches by university presidents on the same afternoon at the same site—a university's auditorium. The first president gave a fine speech based on his knowledge of philosophical issues as applied to everyday challenges in higher education. The second speaker gave an acceptable, but not outstanding speech. It was delivered in a personable and caring manner. The two men left the speakers' platform at the same time. The first speaker hurriedly moved down the aisle without acknowledging persons on either side of the aisle. The second speaker spent a half hour or so talking to, listening to, and sharing his warmth with interested persons on both sides of the aisle. I was somewhat surprised at the luncheon that followed when conversation after conversation centered on the warm and caring leadership of the second speaker. The first speaker's love for ideas was no substitute for a caring exit ritual.

Listening

The two snapshots that follow take you, the reader, backstage into the lives of two leaders, one who is a poor listener and the other who is a good listener. You will see from these snapshots how important listening can be in establishing your credibility as a leader. Snapshot 1.3 portrays a distracted principal who is a poor listener. Snapshot 1.4 introduces us to a principal whose true listening ability is a real source of power.

Snapshot 1.3   Portrait of a High Flyer

Jeff was identified as a "high flyer" from the time he was named an assistant principal. He knew how to get and keep the attention of the superintendent and board of education. He was definitely going places in a hurry.

After a year as assistant principal, he was promoted to a principalship in what was considered an excellent school. The one problem that many educators in the system associated with Jeff was his poor listening. If you were talking with him in a public setting, Jeff was always looking over your shoulder to see if he should be talking with someone else—a person with more power and higher status. It was really quite embarrassing, for Jeff would abruptly end the conversation and bolt toward the more important person.

Snapshot 1.4   Portrait of a True Listener

Dwight was an articulate, well-dressed principal who was liked by everyone. He was one of the most personable and social persons in the school system.

Somewhere along the line, Dwight had learned the value of true listening. When principals in the urban school system met with spouses or friends at social gatherings, Dwight always seemed to be in the middle of the action—listening and rarely talking.

When Dwight walked down the hall of his school, teachers, their assistants, and students would suddenly appear in order to talk to Dwight. He always seemed to have time to meet with them.

Listening is probably the most powerful table manner of leadership available to the educator. It is flattering to the speaker and it demonstrates that you aren't self-centered, but instead are eager to learn more about the person speaking. By focusing on the speaker you will also lessen your anxiety (Linver, 1978). By actively listening you will communicate that you understand where the speaker is coming from, and care enough about that person to step into his or her shoes (Linver, 1978). Make no mistake about it, listening is hard work—what M. Scott Peck has called a manifestation of love (Peck, 1978). It relies on the discipline of bracketing, "the temporary giving up or setting aside of one's own prejudices, frames of reference and desires" (Peck, 1978, p. 128). The true listener temporarily communicates total acceptance of the speaker, the result being that the person speaking will feel less threatened and will make himself or herself more vulnerable by telling you more (Peck, 1978). Richard Amme (2003a), media consultant, also reminds us that focusing our attention, a key to good listening, can be achieved by leaning forward and looking directly into the eyes of the person talking. This will keep your mind from wandering and encourage the speaker to say more.

One of the driving forces that can help each of us become true listeners is our desire to learn more about the person speaking and the subject of the conversation. The good listener, therefore, often stimulates conversation by asking a good question.

The true listener understands the power of seeing self as learner. It is important to add that listening has both a personal face and an organizational face. The true listener can personally profit from the experience, and the organization will also benefit from what the listener has learned and the good organizational impression this makes on the speaker(s). In Goffman's words, true listening is *dramatic realization*, for the listener has mobilized his or her activity to demonstrate that the leader and organization care about learning and the ideas of others (Goffman, 1959). Goffman believes that a member of a *team* uses listening as a way to help others see that cooperation is essential and the task to be performed is more important than the characteristics of the performer (Goffman, 1959). Sarason (1972) also highlights the value of listening as learning communities are created.

Jeff's narcissism and intense drive for a higher position, as described in Snapshot 1.3, may well lead to political payoff but at a price to others and himself: "Politicians strike me as a lonely crowd, making few deep friendships because almost every relationship is tainted by the calculus of power: How will this help me?" (Smith, 1988, p. 92). Dwight, on the other hand, may well achieve a higher position but at a slower rate. My guess is that he will enjoy the journey more and find the love of learning a lifelong benefit.

Avoiding Cognitive Distortions

Distortions in our thinking may occur as we listen and interpret what we hear and don't hear. The secret is to identify these distortions so that we don't act them out. David Burns (1980), author of *Feeling Good*, has identified ten cognitive distortions:

1. *All-or-nothing thinking* refers to your "tendency to evaluate your personal qualities in extreme, black-or-white categories" (Burns, 1980, p. 31). A disappointed candidate for a principalship demonstrated this cognitive fallacy: "Because I didn't get the principalship, I know I just don't have what it takes."

2. *Overgeneralization* is to "arbitrarily conclude that one thing that happened to you once will occur over and over again" (Burns, 1980, p. 32). A newly appointed assistant principal shared her disappointment in leading her first seminar at a nearby university: "This is the first and last time I am going to teach university students. I was a good university student but I am no professor."

3. A *mental filter* is in place when "you pick out a negative detail in any situation and dwell on it exclusively, thus perceiving that the whole situation is negative" (Burns, 1980, p. 33). A newly appointed principal said, "I have a lot of left-brained people on my faculty. The one time I tried a more right-brained approach to curriculum leadership it didn't work. I don't want to take a chance on using this new approach again."

4. *Disqualifying the positive* takes place when "you don't just ignore positive experiences, you cleverly and swiftly turn them into their nightmarish opposite" (Burns, 1980, p. 34). "Thanks for the compliment about my leadership, but you're just being nice" is an example of this kind of cognitive distortion.

5. *Jumping to conclusions* exists when "you automatically jump to a conclusion that is not justified by the facts of the situation" (Burns, 1980, p. 35). This is a kind of *mind reading* because "you make the assumption that other people are looking down on you and you're so convinced about this that you don't even bother to check it out" (Burns, 1980, p. 35). A teacher-leader said, "I know that our school can't implement this new, broader definition of 'curriculum' because the faculty simply won't buy it."

6. *Magnification and minimization* occur when "you are either blowing things up out of proportion or shrinking them" (Burns, 1980, p. 36). "If our faculty sends this e-mail to the superintendent, she will think I'm a terrible principal" is an example of magnification. "The superintendent won't even notice this e-mail from the faculty, she is so busy" demonstrates minimization.

7. *Emotional reasoning* exists when "you take your emotions as evidence of the truth" (Burns, 1980, p. 37): "I really feel guilty

about not being a curriculum leader in the principalship. I know I should be more involved in curriculum and instruction." One problem with this cognitive distortion is that you don't just get on with being a curriculum leader but instead wallow in the guilt.

8. *Should statements* are an attempt to "try to motivate yourself by saying, 'I should do this or that'" (Burns, 1980, p. 37). "I should be a better speaker at parent-teacher meetings" serves as an example. These statements once again lead to one's simply being stuck in guilt.

9. *Labeling and mislabeling* create "a completely negative self-image based on your errors" (Burns, 1980, p. 38). I have often heard school and school-system leaders say, "I never have been a scholar. I'm an administrator—a people person." This kind of cognitive distortion narrowly defines the role of the scholar.

10. *Personalization* confuses "influence with control over others" (Burns, 1980, p. 39). "I never will forgive myself for letting a parent throw a pie in the superintendent's face at our school carnival," said an elementary-school principal. The superintendent took this unexpected event in stride and knew that the principal couldn't have controlled the situation anyway.

All of these cognitive distortions have their holders "paying interest on a debt they don't owe" and in the process wasting personal and professional resources that could be better allocated elsewhere. Educational leaders who have used this ten-point framework find it useful both in school and out-of-school matters, such as friendship and marriages. Several of these leaders have used the framework in giving workshops for educators and parents involved in school and school-system matters.

Speaking

Effective speaking is a major table manner of leadership— one that is given too little attention in most of the formal coursework offered by colleges and universities in general and teacher and administrator preparation programs in particular. Yet it is precisely this table manner of leadership that establishes or fails to establish a leader's credibility. The following snapshot demonstrates the struggle a leader had in achieving comfort and competence as a public speaker. (See Appendix K for an exercise on how focusing on the message relieves nervousness.)

Snapshot 1.5   Challenge of Learning to Speak Well

Lee came from a family that valued informal conversations, but she shied away from formal speaking opportunities. Part of this shyness was because Lee's older sister was known for her speaking ability in a variety of school and university settings. Her sister was president of the senior class and valedictorian.

Lee also believed that her informal speaking ability had to be distinctly different from what was called for in more formal settings. She was wary of standing behind a podium and using a microphone and therefore used a number of excuses to avoid such situations.

Lee's leadership skills were recognized by a principal who became her mentor and outspoken advocate. As a result, Lee moved through the ranks from teacher to teacher-leader to assistant principal to principal of a large high school. Lee knew that she would face many public speaking opportunities and challenges if she moved ahead into superintendent positions—something that she screwed her courage up enough to discuss with her mentor.

Her mentor convinced Lee that she could use her informal speaking style in formal situations. She could be wired with a microphone and didn't have to stand behind the podium. In fact, her willingness to move toward the audience could be seen as an asset rather than a liability.

As Lee experimented with her new freedom to be herself in formal situations, she gained a sense of comfort and confidence and wondered why during all of these years she had so narrowly defined her role as a speaker. She referred to this as paying interest on a debt she didn't owe.

Speaking is a critical communicative skill that can be important in learning more about yourself and others—much as it was for Lee in the snapshot. How significant is this skill in comparison to writing? Sandy Linver (1978), author of the best-selling book *Speakeasy,* answers this question: "The way we interact with other people—both personally and professionally, has little to do with the written word. It is almost totally based on speaking" (p. 18).

There is no one right speaking style, as the snapshot of Lee demonstrates. It therefore makes sense that the starting place is to know what kind of person you basically are.

Please take a moment to complete the following self-inventory. It will give you a start in assessing your *comfort* and *proficiency* as a speaker.

How Good and Comfortable Are You as a Public Speaker?
    Please assess your comfort and proficiency on the following items, from 1 (low) to 5 (high):

Comfort Proficiency

1. Speaking one-to-one

2. Answering questions one-to-one

3. Speaking to a small group

4. Answering questions after speaking to a small group

5. Speaking to a large group

6. Answering questions after speaking to a large group

7. Telephone interviews

8. Radio interviews

9. Television interviews at the station

10. Television interviews in the field

11. Newspaper reporter interviews

Are you more comfortable relating to people in formal or informal situations? If your style is more formal, use a podium and stick rather closely to your detailed notes or written speech. If your style is more informal, as with Lee in the snapshot, leave the lectern and move into the audience as if you were having a conversation. Once again, draw on your "honesty and courage to be authentic with your audience and project to them who you really are" (Linver, 1978, p. 59). Remember that Goffman (1959) reserved the term *sincere* for persons "who believe in the impression fostered by their own performance" (p. 18). A person is cynical if he doesn't believe in his own performances and isn't concerned with his audience's beliefs (Goffman, 1959). One of the best examples of authentic responses was reported in *Time* magazine on January 4, 1993 (p. 55). Television brought the devastation of the Los Angeles riots into every living room, and an unsophisticated man, Rodney King, stepped before the camera and said, "Can we all get along?" It was the TV moment of the year.

Regardless of your style, the secret is to focus on the audience, rather than yourself, and share your warmth with them. One good way to focus on the audience is to think about how curious you are to learn more about them and their reactions to your ideas. You will discover that "it's this desire for contact, to make something happen, that gives a speaker energy" (Linver, 1978, p. 41). One way to share your warmth is to share your sense of humor. This has the effect of relaxing the audience, whether it is one person or 100.

My father attended a college alumni meeting in Sarasota, Florida, hundreds of miles away from his alma mater, Albion College, in Michigan. The speaker was the president of the college. My father called me after the speech and raved about the president. "Why did you like him so much?" I asked. He responded, "He talked to me *before* the speech about my personal interests in the college and he listened to what I had to say." In short, the president set the stage for his own success before he even spoke a word in the more formal setting. The impression that he made on an alumnus remained in this person's mind as he sat in the audience listening to the college president's speech.

The physical setting in which you speak sets the stage for your speaking. In both formal and informal settings, it can be useful to have a mental checklist. For example, remove distractions, such as a gurgling coffeepot; have chairs and/or tables arranged the way you want them; assess acoustics and check equipment; and have a résumé for the person who is introducing you. Goffman refers to such matters as *expressive control*. Your preparation sends the message, "I care enough about you, the audience, to have done my homework." Good preparation also gives you, the speaker, a sense of security.

You will naturally be nervous to some extent before speaking in many situations. Treat this nervousness as a good thing, for it means that you care enough about the audience and yourself to get psyched up for the occasion. Self-talk can be helpful as you prepare: "Good going. I have an edge on and I know that this is necessary in order to do a good job." It is especially helpful to realize that the audience wants you to succeed and is therefore with you from the start. Success breeds success. The challenge is to be interesting to your audience *and* yourself. When you meet this challenge you will experience one of the feelings associated with success: You and the audience will have an interest connection, a sense of oneness.

Twenty years ago I started giving leadership seminars across the country and didn't have much of a clue as to what worked and what didn't. I also didn't know how to deal with my nervousness and excessive energy. As a result, it often felt as if my wheels were spinning. With time, the following learnings gave me enough energy to convey my desire to be with the audience without having so much energy that it made the audience, and therefore me, too nervous.

First, I always wanted to see and therefore experience the physical setting where the seminar would be held the night before it took place. Size of the room, kind of seats, seating arrangements, audiovisual equipment, electrical outlets, flip charts to write on, acoustics, sound from the rooms next door, lighting, and location of bathrooms were important considerations. This gave me the opportunity to work with hotel managers to avoid problems and, perhaps more important, I could clearly see an image of the seminar room ten hours or so before the daylong seminar would take place. On one occasion about five years into my seminars on leadership, I was asked to speak to a small group the night before the main event the next day. It was basically a book autographing party. At the end of this evening speech, I asked any participants who were planning to attend the next day's seminar to meet with me for a few minutes. A simple question addressed to this group turned a brief session into an hour's discussion: "What do you like and not like about leadership seminars you have experienced in your career?" One participant's response was unanimously supported by the other ten people in this gathering:

> I am tired of speakers who simply entertain us with a "dog and pony show." These speakers are "show dogs" who seem to be less interested in the subject matter than they are with their own inflated egos. *We hope that you will engage us with the subject matter tomorrow.*

After hearing this request, I was shaking in my boots. I had spent five years sharpening my leadership seminar presentation of self and with each year the end-of-seminar evaluations of my presentation got higher and higher. I knew that my only hope for success in meeting my small group's advice was to pull an all-nighter to rework the seminar for the next day. I sat down at my hotel-room desk and became completely engaged with the subject matter for the next day's seminar and how this change in focus would speak to the audience. It was more important to get behind the eyes of the participants than it was to feed my own ego and get high end-of-seminar evaluation grades. There were several results of this change of focus in the seminar the next day. My presentation of self was less slick—indeed even clumsy at times—and I had less confidence than I would have had if following the established way of doing things. At the same time, my inner compass gave me the good feeling of knowing that I was more on track with the students' needs and desires. Evaluations for the seminar yielded lower numerical scores. I would have given myself a C+ at best in spite of my increased effort. A real benefit with time was that by focusing less on myself I saw myself as part of a much larger and more important matter—the learning setting and opportunities for participants *and* me to learn and grow. This perspective eventually led to decreased nervousness as a seminar leader.

The second thing I learned to do in preparation for leadership seminars was to set up a desk area in my hotel room so that I had a working area in my home away from home. Books and photocopied seminar materials were spread out on the desk and any table space available. Further preparation for the seminar presentation could be done in this study area. I reminded myself that having a passion for the subject matter of the seminar was the key factor in achieving success the next day. Early in my seminar-leading career, I discovered that I would probably wake up during the night in anticipation of the next day's events. At first, I tried to force myself to go back to sleep, but it soon became clear that it was better simply to move to my study area and further prepare for the next day. After an hour or so, my nervousness subsided, thanks to immersion in subject matter, and I would sleep reasonably well. In the event that I was doing a seminar in my hometown, I simply used my home study area as an oasis to prepare for the next day's seminar.

Third, several years into my seminar's presentation, I began to understand the power of anecdotes and stories. From the time I was a young child, the subject matter of my life was observing other people—often in humorous situations. Interestingly enough, these stories began making their way into my seminar presentations to illustrate points being made.

At first, it was somewhat of a surprise to me to hear positive audience reaction to these stories. With each telling of a story, greater precision of emphasis and word choice emerged. It was almost as if the stories carried the seminars from point to point. Motivated by this knowledge, I became more observant in airports, shopping malls, religious gatherings, and university settings. All of these situations provided grist for the mill of my speaking and writing.

Fourth, it was important to get to the seminar room the next morning at least two hours in advance of the seminar presentation. This gave me a chance to get chairs and tables in place, audiovisual equipment in working order, handouts in front of each chair, and the like. It was also a good time to greet as many participants as possible to establish an affinity connection and lessen my nervousness. Fifth, and finally, I reminded myself that I was an important part, but only a part, of the seminar activities. Many others participated in the preparation for this event—including those who invited me, the hotel management and staff, and especially the participants who invested their time and money to attend the seminar. "I have done all that I can to this point, seminars have been successful in the past, and the audience wants this to be a good day or they wouldn't have invited me and attended the seminar," I said to myself.

One of the advantages speaking has over writing is that you get immediate reaction to your ideas. Since much of communication is nonverbal body language, you will be able to read your audience and know how your ideas are being received. As you share your warmth with them, they will share their warmth with you. Speaking situations also give you the opportunity to revise ideas while you are on your feet—a kind of artistry in action.

It must be added that principals and other educational administrators sometimes experience a school or educational setting in crisis and a reporter arrives to interview the leader about a dangerous, controversial, or devastating issue that calls for a calm and concerned response. You must realize that you and the reporter have different agendas. You want your school system, your school, and yourself to look good, but the reporter is focused on the abnormal. In fact, the reporter's career depends on getting the unusual story's details "wall to wall." Not only that, but the reporter is racing against other reporters to get the story first (Amme, 2003c).

It is important that you know the message you want to send. This message must focus first and foremost on the parents' primary concern: "Is my child safe?" A high school had a series of incidents that brought media attention to its campus: Two teachers had sexual relations with students over a period of several months, fights broke out in the school over racial issues, and athletes were kicked off of teams for drug use. The principal articulated his message several times during interviews: "We vow to keep your children safe!" The next day's newspaper headlines read, SCHOOL VOWS TO PROTECT ITS STUDENTS! This high school principal was also wise to respond in a timely manner. Some educators wait too long to respond, hoping that the controversial matter will go away.

It is important when managing a crisis that internal communication within the school and school system be given a good deal of attention, rather than simply focusing on external communication. One school system blanketed audiences within the school system with e-mails, letters, and phone calls after an incident and then also put information concerning the controversial issue on the Internet. Their crisis management consultant told me that 80 percent of their communication was internal because he believed that each educator within the school system was a significant voice who could influence persons outside of the school system. He also advised educators being interviewed to be able to articulate a genuine apology when appropriate, as this would take the wind out of the reporter's sails.

Dealing with all of these matters affords the leader the opportunity to gain experience that will be invaluable in future decision-making situations.

Because more and more educators are expected to go on television, the following list of guidelines may be useful to you in meeting this challenge:

1. Talk to the reporter, not the camera or microphone. Look the reporter straight in the eye.

2. Stand or sit erectly. Don't stoop or bend over.

3. If you say "No comment," add that you will get back to the reporter by such and such a time.

4. Know who you're dealing with and develop rapport with the reporter when possible.

5. Remember that the good photographer (camera person) doesn't necessarily have the camera to his or her eye. The camera can be rolling from any position, even if it is under his or her arm.

6. Be politely on your guard all of the time.

7. Take advantage of nonconfrontational "good news" programs.

8. The bottom line is to meet reporters head-on and be honest. The camera doesn't lie. It will see your eyes.

9. Be cool and confident. It disarms reporters.

10. Remember that there is a high degree of sensitivity about minorities and women at this time in the history of our nation.

11. A smile is the most disarming thing in the world. Bring to the camera the real person inside you.

12. Be prepared. If you don't know, say, "I don't know."

13. There is no such thing as "off the record." Beware of the reporter who says, "This is off the record."

14. You can ask to talk to the reporter about something before you go on camera. If the reporter won't allow you to do this, don't proceed with the interview.

15. It is a good idea to suggest a place for the interview. Get an appropriate visual backdrop.

16. Watch hazards around you. Don't swivel in a chair. Don't fidget. Calm down, even if it means that you grab a desk in front of you or behind you.

17. Take your time.

18. Ask to reshoot if you are extremely dissatisfied with the interview.

19. Limit the number of remarks and focus on two or three major points.

20. Ask the reporter not only who he or she has already talked to, but who else will be talked to before this story is over.

21. You can occasionally stop a reporter dead in his or her tracks by saying, "I have no earthly idea what you're talking about."

22. Be alert to the fact that some reporters may practice the "'wouldn't you say' school of journalism" (Schieffer, 2003, p. 51). A reporter may ask, "Would you say that your school has serious security problems?" If you even nod yes, you may well be quoted as saying, "The principal says his school has serious security problems!"

23. The school or central office is "private" property. Be aware, however, that television cameras can "shoot" onto your property from a nearby site without your permission.

All of these suggestions are examples of what Goffman calls *impression management* (Goffman, 1959). Familiarity with television interviews will be enhanced as you have more and more experiences with reporters. How does one get better and better at this? Practice . . . practice . . . practice. "Winston Churchill was asked what he did in his spare time. He responded, 'I rehearse my extemporaneous speeches'" (Adams, 1983, p. 229).

Writing

Writing affords you another vehicle or tool for communicating with parents and others interested in schools and school systems. Time and time again, parents share with others memos, letters, e-mails, and newsletters from the principal's office that have serious spelling and grammatical errors. Teachers' comments on student papers also sometimes have such errors. Parents ask, "How can they teach good writing when they don't know what good writing is?"

Correct spelling and grammar are important table manners of leadership. Because we all make spelling and grammatical errors at times, the secret is to have a proficient copy editor who will proofread your memos and the like. It takes extra effort and time to use a proofreader, but many an embarrassing moment can be avoided by such effort.

An important question to ask in sending an e-mail, letter, or memorandum is, "What is my purpose in doing this?" This purpose should be clearly stated, with concrete next steps spelled out concisely and precisely, so that colleagues, parents, or other adults know what they are expected to do after reading the communication. In the event that you want to expedite such a response, ask for it (with an e-mail) or include a stamped, self-addressed envelope with a memo or letter.

Finally, send clean copy. Poorly typed communications and badly photocopied materials send the message that you are sloppy and unprofessional.

Writing affords the teacher leader, principal, central-office leader, and superintendent the opportunity to "stimulate reflective thinking" (Gordon, 2004, p. 149). Many administrators have attended seminars where doing autobiography and journaling are used to think through and then express the patterns and principles in their professional experiences (see Appendices A and C). The "know thyself" dimension of professional development helps the educational leader construct meaning—the foundation of understanding from which emerge the leader's core values.

Miscellaneous Table Manners of Leadership

More traditional methods of communication, such as the telephone, as well as modern methods like e-mails and voice mails afford the educational leader the opportunity to use the table manners of leadership. The following guidelines may be useful to you as a leader:

1. When leaving a message on voice mail or a telephone answering machine, state your name, telephone number, nature of the business, and the best time to return the call. *State this information slowly.* Remember, the person listening to your request is writing the information down.

2. Before meeting with other persons or having important phone conversations, prepare for the content of the conversation, even if this means writing notes from which you speak.

3. Always give your full name when making a phone call. Some people begin speaking and the other party has no idea who it is.

4. There are two major ways to assure you that you can do something with the support of your "bureaucratic superiors": (a) remove irritants and (b) be willing to share the credit if efforts are successful, and share the blame if they are not. Many of the irritants that arise emerge from problems associated with e-mails and telephone conversations. Attention to seemingly insignificant matters can pay rich dividends in the long run.

5. When substantive agreements are arrived at over the telephone, follow up with an e-mail or memo of understanding, concluding with, "Unless I hear from you otherwise, I'll assume this is correct."

6. Log important contacts with other parties.

7. Choose your "battles" carefully. Don't sweat the small stuff. To do so makes you run the risk of goal displacement. Your original, important goals are displaced by minor matters.

Note: See Appendix L for guidelines on the table manners of graduate school leadership. These guidelines may help graduate students avoid the many pitfalls facing them.

CONCLUDING ADVICE
FROM A POLITICAL PROFESSIONAL

Robert Reich (1997), Secretary of Labor in the first Clinton administration, has written a fascinating book titled *Locked in the Cabinet.* It is one of the finest books I have read on the presentation of self and leadership in large institutions, in this case largely political ones. Secretary Reich was given a list of tips by his advance man, Ken Sain, a veteran of many political campaigns. Sain referred to this as his *muck list,* by which he meant his "to do list" for people who are high muckety-mucks—in this case, a list for Reich as a cabinet member:

> *First,* you must immediately hand off all briefcases, luggage, tote bags, and carryalls. A muck doesn't carry bags. *Second,* you must go directly through doorways without waiting for others to go first. The *third* principle is you walk quickly, with head held high and back straight. A muck always looks like he's late for a meeting with the President. *Fourth,* always wear suits that are pressed, shirts freshly cleaned and pressed, and shoes that are shined. *Fifth,* get in the camera shot. No use looking like a muck if they don't see you. There's one exception that I'll get to in a moment. *Sixth,* when you're invited to give a speech, always arrive in the nick of time. Better yet, be a few minutes late. A muck lets his host *worry* just a bit.

Seventh, when you've finished speaking, *don't* sit down at the head table. You'll have to listen to the other speakers. A muck doesn't listen to other speakers unless they outrank him. Leave immediately, or work the room and then exit. *Eighth,* when you work a room, spend no more than five seconds per handshake. Grab their hand before they grab yours, so that you're in control of the grip and can quickly move on. Make eye contact but maintain peripheral vision so you know where you're heading. *Ninth,* when walking in public with the President or Vice President, trail slightly behind them— even when they're talking to you. When they're making a speech, stand behind and to the side and look as though you're interested in every word. Never get in *their* camera shot. A muck always shows respect to higher mucks. The *tenth* and final rule of muck-dom is the most important. Whenever in public—in an airport, on the street, wherever—always look *cool.* Don't frown. Don't clown. Don't be down. A true muck is always in charge. (pp. 126–127)

Robert Reich told Ken Sain that it would take him years to learn all of this, after which Sain said that he would get the hang of it and then face the biggest challenge of all: "Unlearning it when you leave the cabinet" (p. 127). Sain laughed. Sain's list for being a successful cabinet member was vintage Goffman—a set of presentation-of-self principles for a particular role.

We would do well to remind ourselves that all forms of communication are promissory activities (Goffman, 1959). We promise that we will act out what we have said we will do.

BARRIERS TO CREATING A CULTURE OF CIVILITIES

We could strike up a conversation with almost any educator on the importance of civilities and there would be mutual agreement as to their importance in the culture of settings and organizations. The expression of simply kindnesses would mean something to participants in this conversation because we have experienced the differences such civilities have made in our lives. I have had such conversations, and we always tell stories of how this person or that did something that made life a little better for us. There is a feeling of goodness and warmth as the stories are told and heard. Why is it, then, that so little attention is given to the civilities of leadership in so many settings?

A story will make clear that this problem is real, after which the barriers to the exercise of civilities in institutions are identified and discussed. During my career, I have had the opportunity to participate in three distance-education doctoral programs in three universities. The setting for the following story is a large, private university whose doctoral program for educational administrators began in January 1972. The nontraditional nature of the program brought immediate and sustained criticism in professional and popular publications. A major factor in countering credibility issues was the fact that the university's faculty of prominent national lecturers would fly in to cluster sites across the nation to conduct a daylong seminar. Although there was a lack of sustained contact with the lecturers, students and the university could claim an adjunct faculty of nationally recognized researchers, scholars, and successful veteran superintendents.

I gave my first lecture for this university in the spring of 1983 as a substitute for a prominent curriculum theorist who became ill with a kidney disease. During the next 12 years I served as a faculty member, followed by eight years as both faculty member and study area head, a position known as senior national lecturer. In spite of sometimes difficult travel considerations, largely due to poor flying weather, the opportunity to take ideas to different parts of the country was both challenging and rewarding. Doctoral students' reactions to the lectures were very helpful in sharpening ideas for my book and article writing. I also became a part of a community of educators interested in leadership education.

In the past couple of years, the doctoral program described previously has undergone major restructuring, with much of its instruction going online. At the end of the 2002–2003 academic year, I joined ten colleagues who left the study area in which we had taught—the largest exodus of faculty members from a study area in the history of the doctoral program. I was one of a majority in this group who not only left the study area but also left the doctoral program as a whole. And now I come to the point of this story, a point that focuses on civilities and exit rituals. None of the 11 people were given as much as a simple, "Thank you for your years of service to the study area and/or doctoral program." In reviewing my numerous files of e-mails, letters, and student evaluations over a 20-year period, I have asked myself and colleagues in higher education and school administration, "How could this happen?" It is their responses that I found most interesting for they speak to barriers to creating a culture of civilities.

Busyness. A superintendent friend who, when told the story above, replied:

> You need to not take this situation personally. Administrators are overwhelmed with busyness. Most people want to climb the ladder of success in administration only to find that they constantly raise the ladder. When you get in the higher positions, you realize that large institutions are never picnics. They are like the ants without the picnics. People constantly harass you with problems that consume your resources.

While in my waning days with the distance-education doctoral program, I sent an e-mail to a high-ranking administrator expressing my appreciation for positive contributions made. The administrator responded at the end of the day from a hotel out West. I was thanked for such a positive message as it was the only positive response to a long list of e-mails.

The lesson learned was that the person I expected a thank you from had received no thank yous that day. The lack-of-civilities problem was one that permeated the culture of the institution. How can you give what you don't get?

Present and Future Focus. A university professor, upon hearing my story, replied,

> I'm not surprised. You and your colleagues who left the study area were history. Most institutions in the United States, particularly distance-education programs, find history annoying. It eats up resources that detract from the problems of today and tomorrow.

This professor reminded me that entrance rituals are much more fun than exit rituals. Saying "hello" is much more promising than "good-bye." Attention to the past is a special problem for newly appointed administrators who have not experienced the study area's past. Although the newly appointed head of the distance-education program introduced some important entrance rituals in order to assess the state of things, the spirit and letter of such measures were quickly set aside when mandated changes were introduced. The program head and newly appointed study area heads focused on the new and improved, "restructuring" as they called it, for they had no investment in the history of the distance-education program. Both a stated vision and rationale for changes were either missing or inadequate.

Arrogance. Robert Reich (1997) suggests that his "Pronoun Test" be used to gauge the culture of an institution (p. 110). Do people refer to "they" and "them" or do they describe the institution as "we" and "us"? As more and more noise entered the distance-education program, there were more references to outside sources that mandated changes without explanation and without the input of those on the firing line—the faculty and mid-level administrators. People who liked the head of the distance-education program saw the source of the mandated changes as the provost. Those who didn't like or understand the head of the program saw the head and provost as one and the same. Some administrators were considered arrogant in their deliberations with faculty. Some faculty members cited this as a major reason for leaving the study areas. Because administrators didn't conduct exit rituals with faculty who left, they were in the dark with regard to such matters.

CONCLUSION

The table manners of leadership are a combination of attitudes, skills, and tools designed to help the educational leader achieve intended outcomes as well as outcomes that emerge from interactions with others. The table manners of leadership can facilitate civil discourse—an essential part of professionalism. Simple kindnesses or civilities can make a difference as we work together in creating learning settings.

It is easy to discount table manners of leadership as simple technical skills, but to do so is a mistake. The most powerful of moral messages frequently contain artistry and clarity of thought. They demonstrate that the speaker or writer has given attention to the details of communication—a compliment to the listener or reader.

Finally, the biggest enemy of many educational leaders is their constant need to be the center of attention in order to have their egos fed. A colleague, coauthor, and friend, Larry Coble, cited former University of North Carolina President William Friday as an example of a leader with fine table manners of leadership. Friday, although incredibly smooth, has an uncanny ability to shift the focal point of attention to the other person(s) when he interacts. He never fails to show his genuine interest and concern through his interpersonal skills while many other leaders project themselves as know-it-alls.

Suggested Readings

Brubaker, D., & Coble, L. D. (2004). *The hidden leader: Leadership lessons on the potential within.* Thousand Oaks, CA: Corwin Press.

Goffman, E. (1959). *The presentation of self in everyday life.* New York: Doubleday Anchor.

Kleinfield, S. (1989). *The hotel.* New York: Simon & Schuster.

Linver, S. (1978). *Speakeasy.* New York: Summit.

Peck, M. S. (1993). *A world waiting to be born: Civility rediscovered.* New York: Bantam.

Sarason, S. B. (1972). *The creation of settings and the future societies.* San Francisco: Jossey-Bass.

2

Teams, Teaming, and the Creation of Educational Settings

Whatever it is that generates the human want for social contact and for companionship, the effect seems to take two forms: a need for an audience before which to try out one's vaunted selves, and a need for teammates with whom to enter into collusive intimacies and backstage relaxation.

Goffman (1959, p. 206)

If it were possible to observe and record what a leader says or does as he goes about forming a core group, several things would become quite obvious. The first is that he thinks in terms of a core group: usually a handful of people who will be closest to him interpersonally and statuswise. They will be "his family."

Sarason (1972, p. 73)

To say that the creation of a setting can be like a work of art is to say that it can involve in an organized way the most productive attributes of the human mind.

Sarason (1972, p. 284)

I t is interesting in leadership seminars to discover participants' attitudes and behaviors with regard to teams and teaming. There is at least one person whose basic disposition makes it very difficult for him or her to join a team. I have heard the following reasons expressed for this—usually in one-to-one conversations with me: "It is simply an inefficient way to get things done. I know what needs to be done and I can do it quicker and better by myself." "I don't want to do the work for those who are unwilling or unable to pull their load. And the slackers get credit for the good work that I do. It isn't fair."

The problem in hearing these comments is that the listener has to admit that there is an element of truth to this story. The Goffman quote that introduces this chapter leads us to the remainder of the story. He points out the very human desire for social contact and companionship. Going it alone does not satisfy this need. The "Lone Ranger" operates within his or her own cocoon or surrounding, not really in touch with others or the environment. "What's in it for me?" becomes the internal mantra.

Our need for an audience that will give us an opportunity to be praised, to try out our vaunted selves, is also acknowledged by Goffman. Moreover, he reminds us that secret understandings, collusive intimacies, are shared by teammates. He adds that backstage relaxation is a need met by our being a member of a team. It is hard to read Goffman's quote without having a smile on one's face. With one sentence, he has caught us at our own game.

Teams and teaming are not good in their own right. Bonnie and Clyde, for example, were a team of notorious bank robbers. Any value judgments related to teams and teaming must focus on the nature of the team process and its purposes. It should be obvious that a team is not needed to perform every task. Also, we must often settle for a workable level of unity rather than teaming.

BENEFITS OF TEAMING

When teams are functioning effectively, they "possess a shared identity, a clear focus, diversity, role clarity, a high level of collaboration, administrative support, effective decision-making strategies and a process of continuous self-assessment" (Gordon, 2004, p. 185). The following snapshot, in the words of a third-grade teaching assistant, is graphic evidence of some of the benefits of teaming. Collaboration among three educators benefits children and the educators themselves. They also trust themselves and the children to be involved in an emerging curriculum.

Snapshot 2.1   A Lesson in Emerging Curriculum, Integrating Curriculum, and Staff Cooperation

---

Ms. Hayes likes to have a pet in the room in order to teach students character development traits of responsibility and caring as well as expanding their science observation skills and reading skills by finding related information in books or on the Internet. Spot, the toad, escaped captivity at the end of last year, and Squirtle the Turtle (named by unanimous vote) has become the new addition to the classroom.

According to one of the turtle books in the room, he or she looked like a Common Musk turtle. He lives in an aquarium in about six inches of water with a brick to climb up on. The pet keeper for the week is in charge of feeding "him" turtle food daily, but his favorite meals are live bugs and worms, which anyone can find and bring in. Our orderly line and bathroom routines are

(Continued)

(Continued)

often gleefully interrupted with shouts of, "We found a cricket [or spider] in the bathroom!"

Running to get tissue for the insect capture, everyone excitedly gives the bug-meal to the pet keeper, and all crowd around the aquarium to watch Squirtle devour the squirming bug or suck up a worm, like spaghetti, with audience responses of "O-o-o" or "Yuk!" So feeding the turtle not only involves keeping Squirtle happy, it provides a live "creepy show" for those who are squeamish, and it even helps keep the bathrooms insect free.

Children in other classrooms who know about Squirtle have delightedly brought in grasshoppers and other live insects found at home and kept alive in good eating condition until brought to school.

One day Mr. Sciandra, another third-grade teacher, brought in a turtle his class had just found on the playground and wanted to know if Ms. Hayes wanted another turtle to live with Squirtle. This happened to interrupt Ms. Hayes's math lesson, but without hesitation and with her characteristic enthusiasm she said, "Let's put him in a bucket of water to see if he'll come out of his shell." At this point the new turtle was only a mud-covered shell with no signs of life.

The underside looked misshapen to me and I thought there was no hope something alive dwelled there. The math lesson continued with the bucket placed in the center of the room so all could witness any signs of life within. Suddenly a child exclaimed, "Look, its head poked out!" Lo and behold, a large, healthy-looking turtle emerged, now cleansed in the water so all could observe its shape and bright coloring.

Matching it to one described in the turtle book, we concluded it was a box turtle. We also learned from that same source that turtles have been on Earth longer than dinosaurs, which Ms. Hayes pointed out fit right into their math lesson that day—using dinosaur ages for adding high numbers.

It was decided Mr. Sciandra should keep the turtle in his room since two turtles wouldn't fit in the aquarium. Ms. Hayes provided an aquarium for him from home. Not a beat was lost in that previous day and much had been gained in so many diverse ways.

CREATING POSITIVE CLASSROOM
AND SCHOOL ENVIRONMENTS

I have used this snapshot or case with hundreds of administrators and teacher-leaders. A principal said,

> The first thing this story does is to tell us something about the positive learning environment in the school. Teachers had the freedom to manage real-life situations that built on the learning experiences of children, and the educators involved helped each other rather than letting walls separate them from each other.

An assistant principal added,

> There was a spirit of cooperation as children and adults capitalized on their curiosity. All of them had the opportunity to increase their respect for the environment, animals, and themselves. There was real freedom to be creative. The constraints of subject-matter areas were set aside in the interest of integrated learning.

Finally, a teacher-leader said, "This team effort taught the children the importance of being responsible and caring—for animals and each other."

What, then, are other benefits of teaming? Being on a team invites members to be proactive and affords the security of a support system. Effective teams can set the agenda for an organization and enrich its culture. A proactive team encourages its members to seize the opportunity to make a positive difference for others and self (Califano, 2004). The creative leader recognizes that the tone for an organization is set by how he or she feels about team building. The leader's value system can be realized as the leader encourages members of an organization to create and maintain productive teams. The creative leader can, with input from teams, introduce and support rituals that create meaning, comfort, and security in the organization. For example, an organizational newsletter can provide people with concise and precise information that articulates vision and a sense of purpose. It can encourage creativity in the organization by citing innovations introduced by various teams, and it can avoid the pitfall of overloading teams with too much miscellaneous information. Teams can emphasize a "we" quality rather than an "I" quality—something that combats much of the narcissism of our society's self-absorption and excessive individualism. As a result, members of teams recognize that every member of the team matters. Finally, teams are practice grounds for emerging future organizational leaders. Team leaders who experience success gain confidence necessary for new leadership challenges. Mentoring opportunities also find fertile ground in an organization that values teams and teaming.

CONNECTING THE CLASSROOM AND SCHOOL WITH THE OUTSIDE WORLD

The next snapshot, also in the words of a third-grade teaching assistant, connects the classroom with the world outside of it and at the same time demonstrates how the classroom is a microcosm of the outside world with regard to teaming. The teacher was not hung up on status roles but involved the teaching assistant as a colleague. The teacher was also interested in equity among students and didn't single out a particular student for elaborate praise.

Snapshot 2.2   Team Members Celebrate Each Other and a Larger Cause Outside of the Classroom

---

A third-grade class had just completed watching the motivational *Math-a-Thon* video, which includes children at St. Jude Research Hospital thanking all who participate in order to raise money to help cure their cancers and other dreaded diseases. Then Patrice

Reaves came into the room to teach the bi-weekly Latin lesson, this time formulated as a "Roman style" picnic to teach the Latin words for the various foods she had brought with her, including juice to represent wine. After showing them how Romans toasted each other, she let them take turns proposing toasts. The first child raised her cup and toasted someone's birthday that day. Patrice echoed the toast ceremonially along with the rest of the class. Dekia stood up, raised her cup, and said, "This toast comes from the bottom of my heart—to the children of St. Jude!" To which Patrice, with no more or less recognition than the first toast, led the children in the repeat toast, "To the children of St. Jude!"

Patrice gave me, a teaching assistant, a passing smile, knowing I'm in charge of the Math-a-Thon at our school, but her equanimity with each child's toast gave no more credit to one over the other.

Patrice, the Latin teacher, and the teaching assistant supported each other and the children with their cooperation and teamwork. This became in effect *a public celebration of team members' common goals—an essential process in team building.* Respect for colleagues' talent and good work is absolutely essential for a team to function well. Notice that Patrice did not play favorites with the children. She didn't say that one toast was her favorite one. To assess the value of each student's toast would have ruined the spirit of the lesson. Children and their teachers demonstrated their love and care for less-fortunate children at St. Jude by connecting what some might call an extracurricular activity with an in-class activity. In this snapshot, as in the previous one, educational leaders were open to the artistry of teaching—capitalizing on the creative attributes of each other and the children. The two snapshots illustrate the Sarason quote at the beginning of this chapter: "To say that the creation of a setting can be like a work of art is to say that it can involve in an organized way the most productive attributes of the human mind" (Sarason, 1972, p. 284).

THE THESIS

Both of these snapshots support the thesis or "big idea" in this chapter: The educational leader's challenge is to help create an environment in which adults and children get together to identify and use their talents so that good things like those portrayed in the two snapshots are not only allowed but encouraged. When you are in such an environment, you know it because of its zeitgeist, what is "in the air." Since the educational leader's learning both in and out of school is so important, it is clear that a person must become a better human being in order to become a better leader.

An educational leader describes his journey in order to understand and accept this chapter's thesis:

> As a child, it was never clear to me whether my parents were poor or if they simply thought they were poor due to living through the Depression and other financially threatening experiences. For example, they would drive an extra mile or so to get a dozen ears of corn ten cents cheaper. My father was hesitant to put more than five gallons of gas in the car because he thought having a full tank would cause him to drive more—probably to get that dozen ears of corn cheaper.
>
> One Christmas, my brother—a year and a half older—and I received some gifts together . . . one desk and two chairs that my father had made himself. It was a mystery to me how he expected us to use these three items. I couldn't imagine doing my homework with my brother staring at me.
>
> In the spring after we received the desk and two chairs, Dad returned from an out-of-town trip with a bonus gift—a new croquet set. We took it to the backyard and opened it. Our approaches to the gift couldn't have been more different. I immediately took the mallets and balls to a flat surface and started playing, after which I placed the wickets near where they were supposed to be.

In the meantime, my brother, Bob, read the rules and drew a picture of where the wickets should go. He then figured out exactly how many hits of the ball it would take to go around the course perfectly.

During our childhood, Bob and I thought the other person was both odd and wrong thinking. "How could anyone think and act like that?" It was only with age and experience as leaders that we began to understand that our learning styles were very different—his left-brain orientation linear and sequential, and my right-brain orientation more random and experiential. Perhaps even more important, *each of us learned that the other's talents were needed on a team.* Bob's attention to systematic thinking and details and my willingness to take risks and immediately get involved could actually support each other when given a common team goal.

The educational leader who is conscious of staff members' diverse learning styles and talents has taken an important initiative in the team-building process. The next step is to help educators see and appreciate the diversity among colleagues and students. A variety of consciousness-raising activities and materials, like the story just told, can be used to do this. The school or school-system leader can publicly acknowledge the important role that others have played in his or her talent development. This example of passing the torch from one generation to another can vividly make the point that we are not alone in developing our talents. *We create each other in the process of creating learning settings.*

Fellow team members and others can play a significant part in identifying and honing our talents. The educational leader is now in a position to help team members see that the public celebration of team members' *use of talents* must be exercised. It's surprising how many leaders fail to take this step. Some have a teeter-totter attitude: If you go up, I go down, and vice versa. Others appear to be insensitive. In fact, the celebration of others' talents and successes makes you and your team look and perform better. Celebration of others' accomplishments is evidence of team members' commitment to each other—*the* essential characteristic of an effective team. Also, it has the side effect of making team members feel less lonely.

Peter Senge (1990) reminds us that most of the important decisions in today's organizations are made in teams that serve as an example for learning in the entire organization, and these teams have three critical dimensions:

- First, there is the need to think insightfully about complex issues. Here teams must learn how to tap the potential for many minds to be more intelligent than one mind. . . .
- Second, there is the need for innovative, coordinated action. The championship sports teams and great jazz ensembles provide metaphors for acting in spontaneous yet coordinated ways. Insights gained are put into action. . . .
- Third, there is the role of team members on other teams. For example, most of the actions of senior teams are actually carried out through other teams. Thus, a learning team continually fosters other learning teams through inculcating the practices and skills of team learning more broadly. (pp. 236–337)

Growing a Team

Peter Senge (1990) uses the term *alignment* to describe a team when it is functioning as a whole rather than as a collection of individuals. An aligned team doesn't waste energy but instead demonstrates "commonality of purpose, a shared vision, and understanding of how to complement one another's efforts" (Senge, 1990, p. 234). And, perhaps most important, a team that is at its best serves as a powerful example for the entire organization. The special nature of a team functioning at its best is described by Bill Russell, the Boston Celtics' star basketball player whose teams won 11 world championships: "It would surround not only me and other Celtics but also the players on the other team, and even the referees" (Russell & Branch, 1979, as cited in Senge, 1990, p. 234).

I recently interviewed Gerald Austin, a former superintendent of schools who is a National Football League (NFL) head referee, on the matter of teaming. Austin's expertise as a team builder is evidenced in the fact that he has worked three Super Bowls. His NFL experiences in team building have important implications for educational leaders—implications that he used in his positions as assistant principal, principal, and superintendent of schools.

Each June, he receives a call from the NFL office in New York City for the assignment of his crew for the coming year. His challenge is to integrate officials into a smoothly functioning team . . . the same task facing educational leaders in our school systems.

Austin has mixed feelings as he deals with the reality of the phone call. He's sad about losing a 24-year veteran umpire who was both friend and roommate. At the same time, he's challenged by the prospect of training the rookie umpire.

The second member of the crew to leave is a seasoned back judge who worked last year's Super Bowl. He brought humor and high energy to the crew. He's being replaced by a second-year official at the beginning stage of his learning cycle.

The third official Austin loses was a rookie just two years ago. While on the team, he made great progress and publicly thanks Austin for his role in training him. He's replaced by a solid ten-year veteran to do things in a way consistent with the culture and traditions of the crew.

Austin reminds himself that head referees, like other leaders, tend to think their way is the best way. He also communicates his belief that meaningful structure, high but realizable expectations, and patience are essential in what he calls "growing into a team."

In short, as an accomplished head NFL referee who has worked three Super Bowls, Gerald Austin uses his talents to help six other referees identify and use their talents. The result is a team of officials who make sure the game's outcome is based on player skill, not unfair advantage.

Austin is fully aware of the similarities between his leadership in team building as a NFL head referee and his work as a superintendent of schools. Audience reaction, a major concern of Goffman (1959), must be dealt with: "How much will I let what other people think affect me?" Austin asks. After acquiring all of the knowledge he can, an NFL official learns to go with his instincts. If he is honestly doing his best, he will communicate his sincerity. If he is consistently wrong, he has to rethink his instincts.

When others challenge the educational leader, or the NFL official, he must reconsider what happened to determine whether he saw or interpreted a situation correctly. He must sort through emotionalism to see if facts have been overlooked.

The educational leader and NFL referee must also attend to detail, for successful planning and implementation are the result of small steps rather than large, dramatic moves. Leaders who neglect detail leave the impression that they are lazy or simply incompetent. Jokes about the educational leader driving the organizational "bus" with its doors and windows open symbolize that leader's lack of attention to detail.

School board members, like football fans, are partial, and it is important for the educational leader to understand the way they react from the heart. An effective leader must be sensitive to the feelings of those he leads and try to make decisions that are rational. Participants in school systems and football fans insist on a high degree of performance predictability, and educational leaders, like officials, are the keepers of many of the symbols, rituals, and traditions that serve as images of predictability.

Educational leaders and NFL officials feel pressed to suspend biases they held before assuming positions of authority. They can no longer "shoot from the hip," for they are expected to give a fair hearing to many and diverse points of view. To play favorites openly and appear not to listen to all concerned is to have one's credibility eroded—a serious risk to the organization as well as the leader.

The test of the educational leader and NFL referee is how much he learns from his mistakes. Learning begins with the question, "What caused me to make this mistake?" This question is followed by, "What other options did I have in reacting to this situation?" Timing is critical in this process. A mistake early in a game or an educational leader's tenure may seem to be of little consequence, but it may prove critical later in the game or at a turning point in the creation of an educational setting. The mettle of leaders or officials is assessed by how they bounce back after a mistake has been pointed out to them. Since all human beings have blind spots, a distinguishing characteristic of effective educational leaders is that they discover ways to know what they don't know and then do something about this deficiency. Leaders who "don't know what they don't know" will be embarrassments to themselves and their organizations. Goffman refers to such persons as performance risks.

Both educational leaders and NFL officials have to be conscious of managing others' impressions of them so that others believe they are credible. One's bearing or demeanor must demonstrate to others that one believes in oneself. Passion for the work at hand indicates the importance of the challenges that face educational leaders and NFL officials. We were often told as children that leadership is a kind of grim responsibility that one engages in to serve others. But though leadership involves hard work and persistence, it is also a creative, playful, and joyful process that serves self as well as others.

FORMATION OF THE CORE GROUP

In the first quote that introduces this chapter, Goffman cites the very human desire for social contact and for companionship that leads to having teammates with whom one can share intimacies and relax backstage (Goffman, 1959). Sarason (1972) believes that the formation of a core group is one of the inevitable early steps in the creation of an educational setting. In the second quote that introduces this chapter, Sarason refers to this handful of people closest to the leader becoming the leader's family. The trusted members of the core group (leadership team) have usually achieved this status because of an experienced history with the leader, and it is assumed that "agreement on values and motivation is seen as surmounting or preventing future difficulties" (Sarason, 1972, p. 74). This is what Goffman (1959) refers to as *idealization*. It isn't "nice" or comfortable, but it is essential for the core group to discuss predictable problems in the honeymoon stage of the creation of an educational setting: "What might go wrong and what will we do about it?"

Gathering information as to what is going on in the culture of the school and/or school system is a natural process. A core group will usually have one or more members who try to avoid controversy at the same time that one or more members seem to look for controversy so they can tell stories about it to the head of the organization and other core group members (Schieffer, 2003, p. 51). These "story tellers" or informants can cut through the details and give you information that is very useful. At the same time, informants who are indiscreet and extend their story telling outside of the core group can be a performance risk. Should that happen, the head of the organization, such as the principal or superintendent, must deal with the problem. This matter can be discussed while a core group is in its honeymoon stage.

It is interesting how generic some of the predictable problems are, as discussed in two elementary-school reform efforts (Brubaker, 1982). There were always more wants or desires than resources, human and nonhuman. Some nonhuman resources, such as chalk in classrooms, were easily obtained. Other resources, such as convention travel money, were more difficult to obtain; and some human resources, such as putting the right person into a position already held by a seasoned veteran, were simply not going to happen in the immediate future.

The question of who would decide what consultant(s) would be hired for a particular role was a thorny one simply not addressed in certain situations. Comfort level in such matters was understood to be more important at times than expertise. Also, the matter of whose names should be on publications and in what order was a special problem, given the egos of university consultants and the reward structures of research universities. More often than not, these predictable problems were not anticipated or dealt with directly when they occurred. Rather, core group members responded to criticisms from each other and those outside of the team with the comment, "We have a communication problem." In other words, disagreements were not treated as substantive matters but rather as a matter of the way we talk and write about things. Sarason summarizes as follows: "Anticipating problems and forging a 'constitution' by which the leader and the core group will be governed are intellectually and interpersonally difficult and demanding processes" (Sarason, 1972, p. 76).

All of us have experienced predictable problems while involved in educational reform efforts. The question is raised, "How should these conflicts be resolved or reconciled?" By the formally appointed leader of the setting—for example, the principal? By the representative body—for instance, team leaders or department chairs? By the core group—often an informal association where individuals' power base may be more important than formal status?

Choosing Core Group Members

This leads us to the subject of how core group members are chosen—an important but often controversial issue as revealed in the following snapshot. The newly appointed superintendent needed to demonstrate more sensitivity to hiring leaders from his former system.

Snapshot 2.3   A Newly Appointed Superintendent Forms a
Core Group

The seven-member school board finally reached a decision as to
the rank order in which they would place three superintendent
candidates for the recently merged school system. The first two
candidates withdrew their names due to divisiveness within
the board, after which the board voted four to three to offer the
position to the third candidate. The third candidate accepted
and named his deputy superintendent, a person from his previous
school system in another part of the country. A few murmurs crit-
icizing this appointment were heard but educators in the system
had experienced this kind of thing before and so nothing much
was made of it.

   The same thing could not be said of the reaction to the superintendent's next recommendation. A high school principal from the
superintendent's former school system, a woman, was put forth as
the superintendent's choice for one of the two assistant superin-
tendencies—in this case to be in charge of secondary education.
Objections were openly voiced by people in the community:
"What's wrong with the people from around here? Why do we have
to go outside for qualified people?" Furthermore, the rumor mill
cranked up again to criticize the superintendent and his recom-
mended assistant superintendent: "What kind of relationship do the
two of them have, anyway?" After some heated school board meetings, the board voted four to three to accept the superintendent's
nomination, but they sent him a clear message that he was not to
hire any more educators from his former school system.

   This snapshot demonstrates the serial nature of most
core group members' appointments. The order in which these
appointments are made often reveals their importance to the
leader. Sarason (1972) reminds us that this not only creates
an insider-outsider arrangement between core group members
and those outside of the core group but also within the core
group itself. That is, the leader appears to favor some core
group members more than others. The leader may easily fall

into the trap of thinking that the positive dynamics of his relationship with *individual* core group members will ensure positive relationships among core group members as a whole. A further potential spin-off is described by a central office educator:

> Several of us joined the new superintendent to become part of the central office leadership team (core group). Because many of us were from out of town, we gravitated toward each other socially and spent Saturday evenings together at different members' houses. After a few months of this we stopped doing this because some of the members' spouses simply didn't get along with each other or with members of our leadership team.

One of the things I learned from this experience is that "a successful team is not always a group of friends" (Schieffer, 2003, p. 127). Bob Schieffer, superb journalist and television newsman, used the 1975 Boston Red Sox team as an example. It was said that when they returned from a road trip they took 25 separate cabs, yet on the field they came together as a pennant-winning team. Schieffer described the CBS Washington bureau in a similar vein:

> The correspondents did not necessarily dislike each other and they were usually cordial, but because of the internal rivalries, professional jealousies and competition for the same stories that develop in large news organizations, there was often an edginess to their relationships and they seldom socialized after work. (p. 127)

The news bureau had such stars as Walter Cronkite, Roger Mudd, Dan Rather, Daniel Schorr, and Marvin Kalb.

Core group members often assume different roles than they held in previous settings where they knew the leader. They therefore struggle to fulfill new roles at the same time that they are trying to figure out where they fit in the setting being created. While doing this, the most obvious characteristics of any core group are in play: "high enthusiasm, sense of mission, the stimulation of novelty, the challenge of personal and professional growth, and the anticipations of the consequences of success" (Sarason, 1972, p. 80). The dynamics of this reality are a test of the leader's ability to achieve cooperation while at the same time capitalizing on the diversity of personalities and talents.

Goffman (1959) advises us at this point by saying that the team (core group) must do certain things in order to define situations. Team members must be united in front of the public so that the official position of the leader and core group members is sustained. Team members must convey their respect for each other. A certain distance from the audience must be kept and the hard work of the core group should be dramatized and in the process the loyalty of team members must be rewarded. Comments and nonverbal signs from the leader are often effective in achieving these ends.

Sustaining the Core Group

The leader and members of the core group (leadership team) are obviously challenged in many ways in order to sustain this community. M. Scott Peck (1987) has created a useful framework with four stages of community or team building: (1) pseudocommunity, (2) chaos, (3) emptiness, and (4) true community.

Pseudocommunity is the stage where members of the core group come together for the first time and generalizations and platitudes about things held in common prevail: "With this kind of leadership, we are bound to succeed." "This place really needs some cleaning up and we are the ones to do it." Anyone who has been to an earth party quickly recalls the spirit of pseudocommunity. Hugs and exaggerated civilities are the order of the day. Yet, with the core group's beginning, everyone on Earth has not been invited and those few who have been often have a sense of entitlement. And, as we have already noted, core group members usually have an idealized vision of what the core group can and will do, with opinions to the contrary not welcomed.

Chaos, the second stage, occurs when individual differences emerge. Dissonant voices surface and must be reckoned with by the leader. Peck (1987) believes that "chaos always centers around well-intentioned but misguided attempts to heal and convert" (p. 90). The leader wants things to be *normal* as different individuals fight to control the agenda. The sheer noisiness of this stage, chaos, leads many leaders to invoke an authoritarian leadership style in order to get things under control. The wise leader knows that it is during this stage that *the constitutional issue* must be faced: What norms or rules will we follow as a core group in order to move forward?

Emptiness is the third stage of team building. It is the most difficult stage in creating community and yet is essential as "the bridge between chaos and community" (Peck, 1987, p. 95). When asked what is meant by emptiness, Peck (1987) simply said that members of a group, in this case a team in the making, "need to empty themselves of barriers to communication" (p. 95). What does Peck mean by barriers to communication? He lists five: (1) Expectations and Preconceptions; (2) Prejudices; (3) Ideology, Theology, and Solutions; (4) The Need to Heal, Convert, Fix, or Solve; and (5) The Need to Control. *Expectations and preconceptions* can be so strongly imprinted in one's mind that emerging realities of the situation are rejected or simply not seen. For example, a middle-school principal wanted to use ideas from a sensitivity workshop for principals that featured storytelling as a vehicle for sharing emotions. The principal placed a box of tissues at each round table in the media center prior to the first faculty meeting of the year. After a brief introduction, the principal described critical incidents of an autobiographical nature, teared up, and reached for tissues from time to time. There was no visible reaction from the audience and not a single tissue was pulled from the boxes at the tables. The newly appointed assistant principal, a student in my university class said to me: "I thought the principal was nuts. I lost much of my respect for the principal after this incident." *Prejudices* are another barrier to communication. I observed this in action when visiting an elementary school principal, a doctoral intern, who was reprimanding a teacher for using an ethnic slur: "How can you talk this way to your students and expect them to respect you?" the principal said while adding, "This language will not be tolerated in our school!" The teacher said, "I didn't say the student was a _____. I said that he was acting like a _____." *Ideology, theology, and solutions* can be presented with such certainty that they serve as a barrier to communication. Although teaching assistants were assigned to every teacher in kindergarten through third-grade classrooms in the state, the principal openly criticized this mandate and said that assistants should be eliminated with the funds going instead to lower class size. Assistants and those who supported them felt discounted and simply avoided the subject when the principal was in their presence. *The need to heal, convert, fix, or solve* can also impede communication. A middle school teacher in a rural area had a center for religion surrounding her desk. Pictures and other religious symbols were openly discussed with her students. The teacher had high credibility with most parents who supported her convictions and the center for religion itself. The principal in the school simply went about his business as if the center didn't exist. As this rural school turned into a suburban school, a reporter and several professors from a nearby university pressured the superintendent to deal with this matter, and the teacher, who was near retirement, took early retirement. *The need to control* is an element common to the previously described communication barriers. A doctoral intern shared the following with me during her mid-career evaluation:

> I took a leadership course last semester and part of this course was having a 360-degree assessment of my leadership style as a principal. I knew that I was well organized but I didn't understand before this evaluation experience that many of my peers considered me to be too controlling. I gradually started listening more and talking less, a first step in dealing with this control issue.

True community is a rare mix of time and place. Once the core group members achieve this state, they decide where to go from there. If the core group is at a place where all agree that there are certain tasks to be performed in the interest of reaching agreed-upon goals, members can immerse themselves in such tasks and problem-solving processes. If members are at the place where they are not in a task-oriented orientation, they may simply enter into conversation and enjoy each other's company. Peck (1987) cautions us not to think that life in true community is easier or more comfortable: "But it is certainly more *lively,* more intense. The agony is actually greater, but so is the joy" (p. 105). When you experience true community as a core group (leadership team), you simply know it.

Another model or map for team or community building is the Dixon (1995) model for organizational learning. This model focuses on the role of information. Her four-step model may be paraphrased as follows when applied to sustaining the core group as a team: (1) the generation of information; (2) the integration of such information into the organizational structure, in this case the core group; (3) the collective interpretation of this information; and (4) the action taken on the basis of the previous three steps. She reminds us that "every step of the cycle must take the collective into account" (Dixon, 1995, p. 1).

An example of the Dixon model in action took place in a rural community school system in the Midwest. Five educational directors in the school system's central office had a retreat at the beginning of the school year to identify and discuss the current issues facing them. One of the issues raised was the wide range of pay scales among central office leaders. Personnel recruited in recent years were placed in significantly higher brackets than those with greater seniority. Gender inequity was a major consideration in the discussion. The group immediately saw the need for *(1) the generation of information.* After expressing feelings of disgruntlement, anger, and resentment, the directors agreed on a meeting the following month. At their second meeting, the directors *(2) integrated a vast amount of information into their deliberations.* Two of the directors with special research and technology skills were charged with preparing charts and graphs to display views of the core group—*(3) collective interpretation of the data.* At the third meeting, the core group decided *(4) what action they would take based on the previous three steps.* They decided to schedule a meeting with the newly appointed superintendent of schools, a woman. At this meeting the directors displayed their data and shared their convictions about a need for a more just salary equity system. The newly appointed superintendent of schools agreed that something needed to be done and promised to take her recommendations to the board of education.

It was the matter of collective interpretation that was central to the directors' deliberations. They followed the four basic assumptions advocated by Dixon: (a) all persons were honestly invited to participate in the generation of information, (b) all directors subscribed to the egalitarian values of speaking openly without coercion and with free expression invited, (c) the size and physical arrangements of the setting allowed for and stimulated interaction among participants, and (d) members of the setting had and used facilitative processes and skills to participate in discussions and decision making.

KEY FEATURES OF THE EDUCATIONAL CHANGE PROCESS FACING TEAM LEADERS

The final section of this chapter identifies questions that must be addressed by team leaders as they create educational settings. Questions are followed by a discussion of key features of the educational change process.

"What is distinctly different about the setting in which you seek to effect a change" (Sarason, 2002, p. 114)? Your answering this question assumes you are willing and prepared to give resources to finding out who has formal and informal power in the setting, what change strategies have been initiated in the past, and what consequences have resulted from such efforts. Personnel turnover is a major issue to explore (Sarason, 2002).

Is the need for a new setting clearly recognized by a substantial element of the old setting? The answer to this question is frequently "No"! If the answer to this question is "Yes," the educational leader's chance of success is obviously much greater, for the gravity system of the proposed setting will welcome the leader and many of the proposed changes. If the educational leader and the core group make clear during the initial stages of setting creation that x, y, and z are strong elements of the old setting that need to be *conserved* and indeed celebrated, members of the old setting will feel that many of their past efforts are appreciated and the educational leader has a balanced view of change and conservation processes. This is especially important for members of the old setting who have seniority: They understand history because they have one. It should be added that educators are wary and weary of educational leaders, particularly outsiders, pushing the most recent fad that such leaders feel will give them credibility for their next career move. Those who call themselves "change agents" convey the idea that they are there to change others without being changed themselves (Sarason, 1972).

Is the need for a new setting openly voiced and therefore initiated by those within the old setting? If the members of the old setting reached the point where they openly voiced their need for a new setting, they probably ran some risk in doing so. If they actually initiated a new setting while being part of the old setting, they clearly bought into the change process. (In many settings, unhappy people are passively aggressive: They don't help those who wish to perpetuate the old setting, but neither do they openly challenge them; instead, they undercut their efforts.) The educational leader needs to identify key persons who have given resources to openly voicing the need for a new setting and taking action in order to initiate the construction of a new setting.

My experience is that the chances of success in creating a new setting are greatly enhanced if the need for a new setting is clearly recognized and voiced by key leaders in the old setting, and if such persons initiate action on behalf of the creation of a new setting. Persons in settings frequently say that they see no need for changes and resent imposed changes.

Do those who initiated the drive toward the creation of a new setting recognize the importance of understanding the history of the setting? If not, they run the risk of counterforces that they never anticipated. A recently appointed department chairperson in a high school wanted to create a new setting involving her seven-member staff. Carried away with her enthusiasm for the new setting, she failed to discover that most staff members were secure in their bureaucratic relationship with the previous chairperson. The less-authoritarian, shared decision-making plan she wanted to initiate was considered a threat, so the new setting had little chance of survival. Not recognizing the history of a setting was brought home to me when a guest arrived at the front door of our house two hours after a party began and said, "Oh, the party has just begun?" I responded, "No, it looks that way to you since you just got here." Have you ever had this feeling about the behavior of a newly appointed principal or superintendent of schools?

Are those interested in creating a new setting clear as to their personal vision; the vision for the new setting, goals, and objectives; as well as the vision, goals, and objectives held by members of the old setting? Oftentimes a person's enthusiasm for the new setting prompts him or her to give attention to activities and change strategies, but neglect vision, goals, and objectives. Total attention to activities and change strategies can lead to a carnival atmosphere, in which events have no common threads or sense of direction. As a result, members of the old setting naturally criticize the new educational leader and core group for mindless activity with no personal meaning for participants. Educational leaders sometimes encounter a situation in which subgroups occupy themselves with activities but the total group seems to lack a rationale for its existence. I recently experienced new leadership, actually managership-by-mandate, in a distance-education program. A number of program and personnel changes were made without conveying any rationale for such changes or an overall vision for what the leaders called a "revamping of the old setting." Not only was participants' morale at a low point, but lack of logistical support for students compounded the problem. For example, supplemental reading materials were not sent to students in a timely manner, and e-mails as well as voice-mails were frequently not answered. It was clear to me that the managers' lack of and/or inability to articulate a sense of direction for the new setting and their not being on top of details for implementing the new setting fed on each other at the expense of all participants.

Do members of the old setting recognize and act upon the understanding that persons generally have unlimited desires, but the setting has limited resources? The educational leader will sometimes discover members of the old setting who believe that just wanting such changes will bring them about. Such persons haven't squarely faced the fact that resources are always limited, and enthusiasm for such changes isn't enough in itself. (How difficult it is for a honeymoon couple to sit down before the honeymoon and discuss what they might not be able to do because of limited resources.) Some problems, such as the need for a few office supplies, are relatively easy to solve. The fact that desires will always outdistance resources is a dilemma that must be reconciled or lived with by educational leaders.

Is the rhetoric of persons in the old setting who indicate support for the creation of the new setting consistent with the degree of commitment they exhibit in their actions? The educational leader will sometimes encounter persons in the old setting whose rhetoric outdistances their commitment to action. A physically active teacher-leader polled faculty members throughout the school to find out if they were interested in becoming members of a nearby athletic club. Since only 15 responses were needed to buy such a group membership, the teacher-leader was happily surprised by the 30 potential members who signed forms of intent. A month later, when dues were supposed to be sent to the athletic club, only five of the 30 had sent in their membership fees. The initial reaction of the teacher-leader, who wanted to create this new setting, which would be beneficial to the health of teachers, was one of bitterness. "Never again," she moaned.

The following Commitment Scale/Hierarchy (Brubaker & Nelson, 1974) may be helpful with regard to this matter:

1. I will sacrifice my life and/or the lives of my family and/or those I dearly love.

2. I will give up the respect of those whom I love and I'll forego my status and professional achievement.

3. I will forego economic security and my career.

4. I will have serious conflicts between what I think should be done and my reluctance to do it. I may have to alter my work style and give up those techniques which had previously been successful and beneficial and learn new ones.

5. I will have to alter some habits with which I'm quite comfortable, thus making my job somewhat more difficult. I will feel uncomfortable from time to time as I'll do things that don't seem to be the best way to do them based on my past experience and present assumptions.

6. It doesn't make any difference as past experience indicates. My choice, therefore, is between Tweedledee and Tweedledum. (p. 102)

The value of this Commitment Scale was shared with me by a principal:

I made a photocopy of the scale and taped it to the side of the file cabinet near my desk but out of the view of people who come into my office to talk to me. When teachers, parents, and others want something to happen, I ask them how committed they are to their idea. When they ask me what I mean by that, I take them through the Commitment Scale. Sometimes I even give them a copy of the scale.

They usually smile and then actually do locate themselves on the scale. Their being asked to commit resources to their rhetoric, to "walk the talk," has a sobering effect on most people.

The reader may initially feel that Levels 1–3 on the Commitment Scale are extreme. However, a second reading of the items will remind you that some students, parents, and others confront the practitioner in an extremely emotionally agitated state only to calm down to Level 4 or 5 when they have vented their feelings and listened to information from the practitioner. The practitioner may also at times feel himself or herself at a higher level of the Commitment Scale before taking more reasonable action.

A teacher-leader described a particular situation as follows:

Each school in our system has a "report card" that tells the public our annual goal, objectives, and plan of action. Our school's major goal was to raise standardized test scores. My class was well on its way to meeting this goal when a new student, a nonreader with low test scores, arrived on the scene from another city. My first reaction was, "Why did I have to get this student? I wish he would move again!" At the same time I realized that I, a good teacher-leader, was exactly the kind of person who could make a difference in his life.

How did the third-grade teacher-leader reconcile this contradiction? First, she was conscious of the pain she was experiencing and recognized that her devotion to a "higher authority" than self—the preciousness of the child—was more important than appearing to be a winner with higher test scores. Second, she decided to do the work necessary to deal with the situation rather than deny its reality. Without being conscious of it, she located her commitment to the child and situation at Level 5, or perhaps Level 4, on the Commitment Scale.

Do leaders who are interested in creating a new setting see their role as a matter of chance or as part of the natural history of events? The emergence of leadership at a particular time in a setting's history is part of the natural evolution of that setting, and yet many leaders fail to see this. Rather, they consider it a matter of chance. The educational leader interested in creating new settings needs to identify and analyze those forces that brought him or her to this position of leadership at this time in the history of the setting. A newly appointed superintendent of schools shared the following story with me:

> It was clear to me that my predecessor simply put in his time the last few years prior to his retirement. As a result, many principals took advantage of this to feather their schools' nests. Policies and guidelines were either violated or simply ignored—particularly with regard to financial matters. When I was appointed, the board of education charged me with cleaning up this mess. I knew that by doing this that my tenure in the position could be limited. And, I also knew that my successor would probably be a "healer" since I would be making some tough decisions that would anger many principals and central office managers.

This superintendent of schools demonstrated in his story that he had a sense of perspective about the history of the old setting, the present, and possible events in the future.

Do leaders who wish to create a new setting act as if members of the old setting want to be invited to play some role in the creation of the new setting? The educational leader interested in creating a new setting may be enticed to think that all members of the old setting don't want to be (or shouldn't be) invited to join in creating the new setting, but in fact all are flattered by the invitation, regardless of whether they make this known publicly. The challenge to the educational leader is to find appropriate and sometimes subtle ways to involve all members in creating the new setting. In this way they assume ownership for the creation of the new setting. "Meeting this challenge is consistent with the definition of creative leadership: using your talents to help others identify and use their talents" (Brubaker, 2004, p. 82).

Do members of the old setting who plan to give leadership to the new setting understand the creation-of-settings concept, or do they view changes in narrower terms—such as a series of discrete decisions and actions? It is important that all who give leadership to the creation of a new setting share a common view of the context or framework in which change and conservation will take place. The creation-of-settings concept provides leaders with such a framework. The educational leader will probably encounter many persons in the old setting who see decisions regarding change and conservation as a series of discrete and often unrelated events.

Do members of the old setting who plan to give leadership to the creation of the new setting think in extreme terms, or do they make finer distinctions? It is easy for persons involved in creating something "new" to think in terms of the good people (those who want to create a new setting) and the bad people (those who oppose the creation of a new setting). In order to be an effective educational leader, one must make finer distinctions that will invite all people with many shades of opinions, especially the dissonant voice, into the creation process.

What are the existing regularities in the setting that will be confronted by proposed regularities as the new setting is created? In order to address this question, Sarason (1996) advises us to imagine that we are "a being from outer space who finds himself and his invisible space platform directly above a school" (p. 96). What are the recurring behaviors that you observe at a fixed time in the day? (The value of asking such a question is that it forces us to ask two more questions: "What is the rationale for the regularity? And what is the universe of alternatives that could be considered? Put another way: Can the existing regularity be understood without considering its relationship to the alternatives of which it is but one possibility?" [Sarason, 1996, p. 96].) In answering these questions, we will discover the extent to which outcomes, expressed and tacit or understood, are consistent.

An example of a regularity is the amount of noise and physical movement that one hears and observes in the room identified as a multipurpose room or a gymnasium. Or, we observe that students during a math lesson sit in desks that are in rows and there is a limited amount of noise and inter-action. The intended outcome of physical education is physical exercise that is good for the students' bodies and minds. Yet, we observe on this day that approximately one third of the students sit in the bleachers fully dressed. Why is this? We see that the students have a variety of notes excusing them from exercising. We observe during the class in which math is being taught that there are very few questions asked by students and yet the intended outcome, as typed in the teacher's lesson plan book, is critical thinking. Why is there a discrepancy between the intended outcome and what is observed in the classroom? We discover that many students in this class are either bored or overwhelmed by the assigned work. We note with these examples that there are *behavioral regularities*, what an individual actually does in a setting, and *programmatic regularities*, behaviors associated with a partic-ular planned course of action(s) within a given time frame. The extent or degree of agreement between the stated or intended programmatic regularity and what individuals actu-ally do is of special interest to the observer. It is also true that any programmatic regularity triggers changes in behavioral regularities.

What can the educational leader interested in creating settings learn from the culture of the existing setting, and how will the proposed setting's culture interface with the existing setting's culture? The history of the setting may be defined as "the way we did things around here." The culture of the existing setting is "the way we do things around here." The proposed setting's culture is in the minds of those who wish to give leadership to its creation. The education leader may find that the concept of cultural imperatives or commands is a useful one. Some examples of such cultural imperatives follow:

1. All buildings have heavy screens to protect windows from vandalism.

2. Doors to bathrooms are locked between classes to curtail vandalism and physical assaults.

3. All buildings have traditional architecture (e.g., 90-degree corners).

4. Adults stand up much of the day, whereas students sit behind desks in most classes, desks that are smaller than those used by adults.

5. Adults ask most of the questions, and students are expected to provide most of the answers.

Three concepts are useful to us as we distance ourselves from the culture of a setting in order to observe and better understand it: symbols, rituals, and myths.

Symbols are concrete expressions of more abstract ideas. A symbol quickly conveys a whole set of emotions. The lectern, for example, symbolizes the positional authority of the teacher. A physical education teacher's warm-up outfit symbolizes an informal leadership style, but the whistle around the physical education teacher's neck symbolizes positional authority of a more formal nature. Common language expressions in a setting also tell us about the culture of the setting. The language used by school psychologists, for example, is quite different from the language used by classroom teachers.

Rituals emerge from human interactions in order to provide persons with the emotional security associated with predictable behavior. Attendance taking and flag ceremonies serve as examples of rituals in educational settings. It is inevitable that rituals will emerge in a setting. The educational leader can evaluate a setting, using rituals as an indicator of cultural imperatives and regularities in a setting's culture. For example, a new high school principal decided to hold monthly faculty meetings in classroom areas of each department. Each department head introduced the faculty meeting with a brief description of its activities.

Myths are "stories" persons in a setting tell to help the person manipulate tensions about interpersonal relationships. They contain elements of reality and unreality, as demonstrated by the myth that "the boss controls everyone in the setting." If we study the setting carefully, we find that there are many and diverse ways, some ingenious, for getting bosses to do what others want them to do. For example, in a school system where the superintendent prided himself on curriculum leadership, as demonstrated by his attendance at curriculum conferences, central office leaders and others used their informal sources of power to influence what conferences the superintendent attended. They prided themselves on their use of such influence.

"Have you built into the change process meetings or forums in which you and the participants review and assess what has happened or has been accomplished or not" (Sarason, 2002, p. 114)? You must be emotionally equipped to consider and discuss in an open forum criticism of what has taken place to date, and you must be able to know the difference and decide what compromises are acceptable and unacceptable. One key to this is "to view conflict not as an evil but as an opportunity for learning and change; not as a sign of failure and therefore to be avoided and suppressed but as an inevitable occurrence that must be confronted" (Sarason, 1972, p. 211). Finally, you must consider what you will do if the compromises are too great, thus leading to the shutdown of the proposed changes (Sarason, 2002):

> Because you know, you certainly should know, that one source of failure of a reform effort is that a person in a key role—such as the principal or superintendent—has

decided to leave, what agreement should you seek that gives you a role in selecting a replacement? (p. 114)

It is best to consider this matter at the front end of the creation of an educational setting and do everything you can with the powers that be to get their endorsement of your role in selecting a replacement for key personnel. It is difficult during this honeymoon period to talk about such issues, since those who endorse the creation of a setting are so absorbed with the goodness of the proposed changes, but it may well be too late to deal with this matter at a later date—especially if the leader(s) who leave used their power base to initiate the reform effort. Your power through association with the leader on his or her way out may be lost along with your own credibility and that of the reform. You may be isolated or even asked to close down the proposed setting and leave.

CONCLUSION

Leaders and leadership teams can make a significant positive difference in the lives of students, fellow educators, parents, and others if they have substantive knowledge of how educational settings can be created—the ways in which civilities can be exercised in order to deal with the problems, dilemmas, and opportunities that face them. As Seymour Sarason says in one of the quotes that introduce this chapter, "To say that the creation of a setting can be like a work of art is to say that it can involve in an organized way the most productive attributes of the human mind" (Sarason, 1972, p. 184).

Finally, what is the relationship between team development and professional development? "Team development is vital to the core function of professional development: the improvement of teaching and learning" (Gordon, 2004, p. 195). "Professional Development on the Presentation of Self and the Creation of Educational Settings" is the title of the following chapter.

SUGGESTED READINGS

Brubaker, D. L., & Coble, L. D. (2005). *The hidden leader: Leadership lessons on the potential within*. Thousand Oaks, CA: Corwin Press.

Dixon, N. (1995). *A practical model for organizational learning*. Greensboro, NC: Center for Creative Leadership Issues and Observations.

Harvey, T. R., & Drolet, B. (2005). *Building teams, building people: Expanding the fifth resource*. Lanham, MD: Scarecrow.

Peck, M. S. (1987). *The different drum*. New York: Simon & Schuster.

Putnam, R. D. (2000). *Bowling alone: The collapse and revival of American community*. New York: Simon & Schuster.

Senge, P. M. (1994). *The fifth discipline: The art and practice of the learning organization*. New York: Doubleday.

3

Professional Development on the Presentation of Self and the Creation of Educational Settings

To help others to change without this being preceded and accompanied by an exquisite awareness of the process in ourselves is "delivering a product or service" which truly has little or no significance for our personal and intellectual growth.

Sarason (1972, p. 122)

The voluntary taking of serious chances is a means for the maintenance and acquisition of character.

Goffman (1967, p. 238)

By most accounts, the brand of inservice training we have been offering teachers and administrators has not proven to be effective for helping them gain the deep content knowledge, classroom management and interpersonal skills, technological know-how, understanding of schools as organizations and other concepts and attitudes required by an increasingly complex educational context.

Betty Fry in Collins (2000, p. ix)

So much of staff development is crammed down our throats.

A Veteran Teacher

This chapter is devoted to ways in which *professional development leaders* can give attention to the presentation of self and the creation of learning settings. The chapter begins with a description of various ways in which professional development is defined. The culture of professional development in a particular school or school system illustrates the way in which professional development is operationally defined. The definitions section of the chapter is followed by an identification and discussion of my basic assumptions underlying professional development. These assumptions spell out my *rationale* for professional development on the presentation of self and the creation of educational settings. Bruce Joyce, a prominent scholar on professional development matters, reminds us that it is incumbent on professional development leaders to provide rationale for what others are asked to do (Sparks, 1998). The final section of the chapter focuses on professional development strategies that can make a difference in helping you and others engage in presentation of self while creating learning settings. A professional development plan that I constructed with a core group of educators is a pilot study of issues that will face you, the reader, as you move forward with your own professional development plan that focuses on the presentation of self and the creation of educational settings. (You may wish to refer to Appendix A for guidelines that will be helpful in writing your professional development leadership plan.)

DEFINITIONS OF PROFESSIONAL DEVELOPMENT

It is good to remind ourselves that the work that educators do while participating in professional development leadership will reflect the ways in which they think about this matter. We therefore begin with ways in which professional development is defined. The title of this chapter has two very powerful words whose definitions tell us a good deal about the basic assumptions held by those who define them. The word *professional* is often used to refer to the positive characteristics of a person who is a highly qualified member of a particular vocation. For example, an educator is current or up to date as to theory and practice and can articulate this knowledge to others; the professional educator is proactive and takes the lead in making things happen and also has good follow-through so that others can count on him or her; and the professional educator has good presentation-of-self skills as well as the ability to create learning settings. At times, the word *professional* is used to emphasize a particular characteristic considered to be more important than all others:

> My surgeon is a real professional who doesn't let feelings and emotions get in the way of performing a service. It's important to have a cool head during surgery. And, a superintendent of schools who gets too emotionally involved doesn't do anyone any good. In order to see the whole picture and deal with tough issues, the superintendent has to keep a certain distance.

The Professional Organizational Model

A second meaning of the word *professional* refers to power arrangements in an organization. The *professional organizational model* is as follows: make the decision, implement the decision, and deal with public reaction. Three characteristics differentiate the professional model from the bureaucratic model: First, the professional organization is primarily concerned with the discovery or application of knowledge. Its basic function cannot be programmed and therefore cannot be carried out efficiently by hierarchical arrangement and compliance with administrative orders. Collaboration and the sharing of knowledge are important (Darling-Hammond, 1997). Second, professional organizations have many nonprofessional and semiprofessional workers who may be organized in the traditional bureaucratic manner, but *basic decisions about functions are made by the professionals themselves* (Cranston, 2000). Third, professional organizations emphasize achievement of goals rather than disciplined compliance with a highly programmed process for achieving objectives (Darling-Hammond, 1997). Processes used in professional organizations can be highly flexible and individualistic, as the professional's judgment dictates.

The professional, according to the professional decision-making model, is bound by a norm of service and a code of ethics to represent the welfare of his or her clients. The professional's source of authority comes from his or her technical competence, expertise, and knowledge. The professional's decisions are governed by internalized professional standards. *The court of last resort for appeal of a decision by a professional is his or her professional colleagues.* Hospitals and research institutes are, perhaps, the best examples of the professional decision-making model, although even these organizations are a mix of professional and bureaucratic forces. The public hospital is dependent on local and/or state and/or federal governments for support, and is accountable to those governments for compliance with their rules and regulations. At the same time, the public hospital provides treatment for its patients within a model more professional than bureaucratic. The medical profession decides who can practice in the hospital, what treatments are appropriate for what patients, and the competence of their colleagues, the medical doctors. Nurses, technicians, and aides are typically organized bureaucratically and are governed by professional decisions made by medical doctors.

The Bureaucratic Organizational Model

In order to understand the professional decision-making model better, we now turn to the *bureaucratic decision-making model:* Anticipate public reaction, make the decision, and implement the decision. This model has the following characteristics:

1. The detailed subdivision of labor, to be performed by many different highly trained specialists;

2. General rules and regulations to ensure objective and impersonal treatment of the organization's clients, and to coordinate the efforts of the organization's specialist workers to promote an orderly, systematic, and rational means of providing services; and

3. Hierarchical relationships designed to ensure the coordination of the specialists' efforts by providing clear and rational allocation of authority and responsibility.

Most schools are organized bureaucratically. Why is this the case? The first reason is that bureaucracy provides for disciplined compliance with rules, regulations, and directives from superiors. There is no need for discourse about who has the authority to make decisions and direct the activities of others. The superintendent clearly has the legal authority to direct the activities of the principal; the principal has the legal authority to direct the activities of the teachers; and the teachers clearly have the legal authority to direct the activities of the students.

Second, the hierarchical organization of a bureaucracy provides clear lines of authority and responsibility so that individuals can readily be held accountable for their actions. In any organization primarily concerned with public reaction, fixing responsibility appears to be essential. Somebody's "head has to roll" when things go wrong.

A third reason is that bureaucracy seems best suited to organizations whose ends are discrete and measurable, whose objectives are clear and generally agreed on, and whose causal relationships between means and ends are readily demonstrable. At the risk of oversimplification, the goal of those who hold power in government is to maintain their power; the means to maintaining that power is favorable public reaction to governmental acts; and the causal relationship between means and ends is obvious: You don't stay in power long if the people don't approve of what you are doing.

Looking Back at the Humanistic Education Era

During what is known as "the humanistic education era" of the 1970s and 1980s, advocates of humanistic education argued that curriculum and instruction decisions should be made in the professional decision-making model (Brubaker, 1982; Brubaker & Nelson, 1974; Zahorik & Brubaker, 1972). Teachers within this professional development model were expected to *develop* curriculum materials for students whenever possible. At the same time, it was acknowledged that bureaucratic organization would continue to be used in order to respond appropriately to public reaction. In effect, there would always be some tension between professional and bureaucratic forces, but this tension could be the friction that lead to creative movement within schools as leaders worked toward a reconciliation of these forces. Constructivism, the development of curriculum materials by teachers and central office curriculum leaders, would lead to the creative feeling of ownership.

TODAY'S MANAGEMENT BY MANDATE

In recent years, external forces, such as federal and state governments, have been heavily engaged in management by mandate—a form of governance clearly in the bureaucratic decision-making model. Although measurement is but one form of assessment or evaluation, politicians and superintendents often talk about measurement to the exclusion of assessment or evaluation. Measurement and high-stakes testing go hand in hand with the accountability referred to frequently in speeches and legislation.

An example of this came to my attention recently when I attended a professional development workshop in a nearby school system. Two representatives from each school in the school district listened to an out-of-state consultant who addressed them as follows:

> Welcome to our workshop on curriculum alignment. Let me begin by defining a few important terms. The *essential curriculum* is the state-mandated curriculum, the course of study. The *tested curriculum* consists of standardized tests mandated by the state. *Curriculum alignment* is the proper adjustment of what is taught, so that the essential curriculum and the tested curriculum are in line with each other.

The remainder of the workshop consisted of a demonstration of how essential curriculum materials constructed by the State Department of Public Instruction were to be used by teachers. Materials were in notebooks with color-coded lesson plans and the like. The effect of this workshop was to shrink the curriculum to fit itself. And, *measurement* of student success, or lack thereof, would yield standardized test data. This approach to curriculum and professional development is very seductive in a nation that worships numbers.

All of the discussion thus far in this chapter simply makes the point that *professional development* in today's public schools takes place within a bureaucratic decision-making context. Lee Shulman says this best:

> The confusion stems from valuing standards, on the one hand, and embodying these standards in high-stakes assessments on the other. The assessments end up corrupting the value of the standards. The standards get modified to be consistent with what we're able to measure in a high-stakes assessment. We have to ratchet down the

standards and squeeze out all of the creative diversity because we want to be able to develop scoring keys that nobody can complain about or challenge. (cited in Tell, 2001, pp. 6, 8)

In short, the culture of today's public schools, the context in which professional development takes place, is a highly bureaucratic decision-making one that must be taken into account by any leader who wants to give attention to the presentation of self and the creation of educational settings. The work done by teachers tells us a good deal about how teachers think, and the context in which teachers do their work strongly influences the way teachers think—and therefore act. A major effect of the increased bureaucratization of schools is that a side effect emerges as a result of almost exclusive attention to increasing students' test scores. Lieberman and Miller (1999) warn us as follows: "In schools that focus primarily on students' learning, teachers often feel overwhelmed and underappreciated, and they cease to take part in the restructuring effort" (p. 12). Teachers have to receive in order to give, and almost exclusive attention on students works against this principle.

PROFESSIONAL DEVELOPMENT REVISITED

The second key word in this chapter's title is *development*. Development refers to the act of bringing out the capabilities or talents of a person. You will notice from the discussion of *professional* thus far that professional development is inextricably linked to two questions: *"Whose development are we talking about?"* and *"Who is primarily responsible for the development process?"*

A simple answer to the first question is that we are talking primarily about the professional development of teachers— those who work most closely with students. (The algebra teacher in the present book's prologue had a presentation-of-self problem.) The answer to the second question is somewhat more complex. Teachers ultimately decide what they will do in the processes of teaching and learning, including their own learning, but they are, as we have seen from the earlier discussion, subjected to many external forces interested in their development: school and school-system administrators, the board of education, federal and state governments, authors and publishers of materials for curriculum and instruction, special interest groups, professional organizations, parents, and students. All of these interactive forces are part of the *context* in which the professional development of teachers takes place. As such, these forces and *their* development are influenced by the professional development of teachers *and others*, including administrators, involved in the process of constructing bridges between where teachers are and where they should be, as well as bridges between teachers and student learning.

BASIC ASSUMPTIONS UNDERLYING PROFESSIONAL DEVELOPMENT

This book began with a prologue about a ninth-grade algebra teacher who lacked the knowledge and skills to present himself effectively to his students' parents. What's more, the principal of the school didn't have in place a professional development plan to address this problem. The principal didn't have or intend to create learning settings focusing on this issue. Once again, professional development has a *personal face* and an *organizational face.* Therefore, the professional development leader has to focus on the psychology of the individual, such as the teacher or the student, and the psychology of the context—one example of which is the school as an organization.

Previous chapters in this book provided *specific information* as to what is involved in effective presentation of self and the creation of educational settings. The thesis or big idea of this chapter is that both the algebra teacher and principal, as well as other educators in this school, would be wise to begin by identifying basic assumptions *they presently share* about effective professional development. Out of this consciousness should emerge assumptions as to *what basic assumptions should* support effective professional development. After assessing human and nonhuman resources available to them, decisions about *what can be done* with respect to professional development on the presentation of self and the creation of educational settings can be made. *What is, what should be,* and *what can be* is always a kind of dialectic in which the educational decision maker engages.

Professional development participants we have surveyed want to know what to expect from their involvement. They want activities related to school vision and the context of the particular school in which they teach. A well-articulated vision provides a sense of purpose and clarity. In order to meet this expectation, professional development leaders must "develop a clear picture of effective professional development" (Collins, 2000, p. xv). This clear picture emerges from the basic assumptions or foundation of beliefs held by the professional development leader.

In the interest of beginning a conversation on these matters, the following basic assumptions are submitted for your consideration.

EDUCATORS HAVE TO GET TO GIVE

It is important to understand and value change in oneself while at the same time focusing on the personal and intellectual growth of others. This is the point that Sarason makes in the quote that introduces this chapter. Any efforts educational leaders make in order to help others create educational settings that improve presentation of self will in turn produce changes within the person who introduces the change. "Do with others" rather than "Do onto others" is the language that captures this idea. To call oneself a "change agent" sends the message that the educational leader is changing others without being changed himself or herself. The leader who strongly values learning will see that entering into a professional development covenant with others will foster a reciprocity of benefits.

Teachers we have surveyed frequently say that they resent staff development that focuses only on student achievement. They want their own growth and development to be considered in professional development activities. In summarizing research he has done on staff development, Bruce Joyce makes it clear that teachers and students need to be partners continuously interested in learning, and they must be presented with the rationale for what they are asked to do (Sparks, 1998). When they experience this, they feel they are receiving as well as giving.

Time and time again, we have experienced professional development *programs* that become so focused on the nuts and bolts of the programs themselves that the personal and intellectual growth of *persons* in the learning setting is given too little attention or forgotten. A mea culpa will illustrate how this can happen. The UNCG Humanistic Education Project was based on the premise that shared decision making is both possible and desirable in our schools. As we began to produce materials for use in classrooms, particularly in book form, we involved only those who had the technical writing skills to produce *a perfect product*. As we took these products to conventions and the like, we created professional development performances or presentations of self that became slicker and slicker. Instead of introducing sessions with an invitation to the audience to question our ideas and products (published materials), we honed our presentation-of-self skills so that less and less questioning of our basic assumptions and products took place. As might be expected, participants' pencil-and-paper assessments of our presentations became higher and higher. Our dog and pony shows created a system diametrically opposed to our intended outcome—shared decision making in general and critical dialogue in particular.

In retrospect, how should we have moved forward with our professional development efforts? We should have built in self-corrective mechanisms as we created products, and we should have introduced and conducted our professional development sessions at conferences and conventions by making it clear that our efforts were simply a *springboard* subject to revision and improvement on the part of participants. Instead of sending the message that, "We are the experts and you are the empty vessels to be filled with our definitive knowledge," we should have communicated that, "We are fellow learners with you in our quest for new understandings." The words and music of what we should have said would have set a tone for our presentation that would have paid rich dividends for all involved—including ourselves, the presenters. The feeling of meaning and ownership experienced by teachers would have been in sharp contrast to the comment of the veteran teacher in the header quote that introduced this chapter: "So much of staff development is crammed down our throats." (See Appendix B for an assessment instrument on what works and doesn't work in doing professional development.)

Curiosity and Passion for Learning Are Contagious

The professional development leader who has "a spark in his (or her) eye," a real interest in the value of the subject at hand, will model this for others, thereby making it more likely that they will be motivated to give resources to the same subject. The audience, to use Goffman's term, reads the professional development leader's presentation of self in the first few minutes of a performance: Does the leader want to be here? Is this subject, the presentation of self and the creation of educational settings, important to the leader or is he or she simply on automatic pilot? Does the leader have a passion for the work (Fried, 1996, 2001)? There is a story in professional development literature that has made the rounds precisely because all of us have experienced its reality. When asked about inservice education, the teacher responds: "I only hope that I die during an inservice workshop because the distinction between life and death will be so subtle."

Staff development participants we have surveyed resent top-down, mandated staff development, often "pulled out of a hat"—to quote an expression they use. The symbol for this kind of professional development experience is *the lecture.* A participant expressed this criticism as follows:

> We are so tired of being told during lectures what we have to learn. Any lecture that lasts longer than 10 minutes is doomed. Lecturers often use standardized topics and leave little, if any, room for questions and discussion. The message is that "one size fits all." There is frequently no input from teachers at any stage of the staff development process.

One-shot, in-and-out staff development, with no purpose and no follow-up or evaluation, leaves many participants with the feeling that "outside experts" are simply in it to collect their money. Consultants who fail to locate their efforts in a research base reinforce this criticism.

VALUABLE PAYOFF A CRITICAL FACTOR

The participant in professional development activities must see a valuable payoff for his or her involvement. Simply getting professional development credits for being there will not sustain the educator's interest. Rather, there must be a connection between the possibility of valuable learning and the content of professional development experiences. At the point where this connection is made, the participant assumes ownership for the shaping of the learning so that it meets the desire of the participant to make a difference. Ideally, the educator as participant loves ideas in general and ideas concerning the presentation of self and the creation of educational settings in particular. To love ideas is to value meaning—something that is frequently lacking in *some* hands-on, make-it-and-take-it workshops: "I've made a puppet, but what do I do with it now that I have it?" Professional development leaders who share real-life stories about educators who have learned and profited from creating educational settings that focus on presentation of self can make a difference in getting and keeping the attention of participants. Improved presentation of one's teaching self that connects with previously unreachable students gets and can keep the attention of participants. Authentic presentation of self on the part of the professional development leader is conveyed to participants by knowing the language of such participants. Goffman refers to this as *audience segregation.* This usually means that the leader has experienced the daily teaching environment of the participants.

RISK-TAKING AND MISTAKE-MAKING ARE KEYS TO LEARNING

The teacher and other educators involved in professional development must be allowed to take risks and make mistakes, from which they learn, in creating settings that focus on the presentation of self. This idea is highlighted in the quote by Goffman in the beginning of this chapter: "The voluntary taking of serious chances is a means for the maintenance and acquisition of character" (Goffman, 1967, p. 238). A professional development program that focuses on the presentation of self will need to provide participants with instructional strategies and learning opportunities that will be personally and professionally challenging. For example, role-playing, videotaping, and real-life experiences will give the participant vivid and detailed feedback as to his or her effectiveness. Educators will literally learn from their mistakes while others watch and critique their performances. It is through practice and more practice that participants will learn to be more accomplished in their presentation of self. Winston Churchill had it right when asked what he did in his spare time: "I rehearse my extemporaneous speeches" (Adams, 1983, p. 229). Professional golfer Gary Player said, "The harder I practice, the luckier I get" (Austin & Brubaker, 1988, p. 105).

Those who take risks need a support system or safety net as they introduce and maintain changes in their leadership in presenting self and creating educational settings. (See Appendix F for an exercise on turning breakdowns [losses] into breakthroughs [victories].) Being mentored, being involved in study teams, and learning while watching more accomplished educational leaders give their performances can be very important. An embedded staff-development model, for example, one that includes a staff development leader in each school to mentor and coach teachers and others, can make a positive difference. The question, "Where is the center of knowledge located?" is answered: "In teachers within our own school." Within each teacher, core values and beliefs are the foundation for everything the teacher does (Fullan, 2001).

PRESENTATION-OF-SELF PROGRAMS TAKE TIME

Professional development leaders and participants must acknowledge and accept the fact that effective programs focusing on the presentation of self take time. There are no quick fixes. Those committed to professional development are in it for the long haul. Not only is it necessary to have time to work in seminar settings where the sharing of ideas and feelings takes place, but there must be time for meetings between mentors/coaches and mentees. Those who are involved in prescribed actions must also be involved in planning since particular actions should be part of coherent, long-term plans. Focus on a community of learners is often novel to some teachers who think of professional development as activities aimed at the individual teacher.

Participants also need time alone in order to read and to reflect on what they are experiencing. Three potential sources for such time have been identified by Collins (2000):

Adding time to your workday and/or contract year in the form of additional "staff development days," rescheduling or reorganizing your time by revising the school's schedule to "find" time during the school day, and utilizing staff in new ways to allow you to spend more time in professional development activities. (pp. 14–15)

Raywid (1993) offers guidelines for allocating and scheduling time for such activities. The activities "should be (1) held when teachers are fresh and capable of active participation, (2) in uninterrupted blocks of time, (3) primarily during the school year, and (4) balanced between regular school days and non-student contact days" (p. 32).

INTEGRATION OF SOURCES OF POWER A KEY TO DECISION MAKING

The professional development participant is wise to give attention to sources of power available to him or her in a particular context. Positional authority is power by virtue of one's position in the organization. It is commonly associated with bureaucratic forms of organization, for those with more positional authority give "commands" to their subordinates who have less. Regardless of the respect, or lack of it, accorded the person with positional authority, the bureaucratic subordinate is expected to obey such commands. Traditionally, positional authority has been drawn upon heavily, but observers in the area of leadership education argue that drawing upon positional authority is much like using a battery: The more you use it, the less there will be to use in the future. They therefore recommend that positional authority should be suspended by the leader where possible (Brubaker & Coble, 2005).

Expertise is a source of power attributed to persons because of their recognized ability to do something well. A lead-teacher in a school may, for example, be recognized as a well-organized person who has demonstrated expertise in writing reports. She is therefore asked to head the accreditation planning team for the school. Or, a professional development leader is a highly skilled networker who taps talent outside of the school without cost to the school. The ability to organize and articulate ideas is a very important kind of expertise essential to the professional development process.

Succorance is an informal kind of power that leaves others with the feeling that they are supported emotionally. It is commonly associated with counseling and coaching. "You can do it" is the message transmitted. Professional development leaders often encounter educators who are ready to give up, due to a lack of interest on the part of committee members or to opposition from a person or group. It is precisely at this point that succorance can give momentum to tasks that must be completed. The morale of the group depends on this kind of support.

Charisma is a sort of magnetic charm. Nonverbal messages, such as smiles or nods of approval, are the vehicles used by charismatic leaders. Style of dress and the leader's bearing give added charisma. Motivational cheerleading can play an important role in helping educators get and keep momentum. The creative professional development leader integrates the sources of power in a manner appropriate for a particular situation. This integration is based on a realistic assessment of the leader's talents as well as the talents of other educators within a particular context. That which the professional leader can and can't do will always depend to a large extent on the bureaucratic voice of those higher up in the organization. In other words, the creative professional leader must be able to read the psychology of the context as well as the psychology of self and other individuals who operate in this context. Tremendous changes in our society in relation to positional authority must also be known and understood by the creative professional development leader. Changes in the world of communication, for example, give all participants in professional development access to information, which means they will not simply accept ideas or do things because the person with authority says so. Children challenge teachers' knowledge bases and teachers challenge administrators' knowledge bases by using their computer skills.

It can be useful for the professional development leader to keep up with recent literature on standards for effective professional development. Work by the National Staff Development

Council, the National Association of Elementary Principals, and the National Association of Secondary Principals can be accessed easily. There is also a proliferation of books on professional development along with articles from such organizations as the Association for the Development of Curriculum Development (ASCD).

I doubt if Joyce Epstein, founder of the Center on School, Family, and Community Partnerships at Johns Hopkins University, would be surprised by the poor presentation of self of the ninth-grade math teacher or the lack of attention to this matter on the part of the teacher's principal described in the cautionary tale at the beginning of this book. Epstein recognizes the important role teachers can and should play in communicating with parents. She also believes that "there must be immediate and dramatic changes in the preservice and advanced education of teachers, administrators, and others who work with schools, families, and students" (Epstein, 2001, p. 18).

One of the changes in the preservice and advanced education of teachers (and administrators) is the need for opportunities to practice talking to parents about what they as professionals do *and* why. (Note: *A major thesis of this book is that the effective professional is able to articulate what she or he is doing and the rationale for such action*.) This is a matter of gaining expertise with regard to the subject matter in the presentation as well as the verbal skills necessary to convey such content. (See Appendix J for a self-assessment instrument on the importance of critique.)

One of the most promising models for schools and school systems to study is Parents and Teachers Talking Together, designed and sponsored by the Prichard Committee for Academic Excellence. This effort, started in 1994 in Kentucky, has trained more than 500 facilitators who have conducted more than 300 sessions to date. The sessions are designed to be a tool for increasing parent involvement in schools. Two basic discussion questions provide focus for discussions between teachers and parents: "What do we want for our students?" and

"What do we need to do to get what we want?" (The reader may read about this program by logging on to the following Internet address: http://www.prichardcommittee.org/pt3.html.)

Local sponsors support each session by:

Choosing a date and time

Identifying two facilitators

Selecting a comfortable meeting site

Inviting parents and teachers to participate

Arranging refreshments or a meal during the session

Setting up the logistics for the event; and

Coordinating the session itself

It is interesting that facilitators address what Sarason (1972) calls "the constitutional issue" at the beginning of each session. Format and ground rules are introduced and the facilitators oversee the discussion process. Each session lasts approximately four hours; information from sessions is compiled on a statewide basis.

The discussion sessions are not an end in themselves, as the Prichard Committee for Academic Excellence is known as Kentucky's best-known education-reform group. This 100-member committee campaigns to get more money for schools and fend off other agencies, including the federal government's No Child Left Behind Act, in its efforts to control state and local school systems.

The following Web sites were helpful to me in my professional development efforts:

National Staff Development Council: www.nsdc.org

Association of Supervision & Curriculum Development: www.ascd.org

National Association of Elementary School Principals: www.naesp.org

National Association of Secondary School Principals: www.nassp.org

American Association of School Administrators: www .aasa.org

PROFESSIONAL DEVELOPMENT PLANS

Reform efforts like those of Joyce Epstein and the Prichard Committee for Academic Excellence are very helpful and yet they don't have the precise focus on educators' presentation of self and the creation of educational settings that is the subject of this book. As a result, ten educators in North Carolina, including myself, decided to give attention to this matter. The purpose of this section of the chapter is to take you, the reader, backstage so that you can profit from our discoveries. Our narrative may well help you develop your own professional development plan concerning the presentation of self and the creation of educational settings.

Step 1: Consciousness Raising. We met for three hours each Tuesday evening over a 15-week period in a seminar setting in order to ensure contact with each other and the subject at hand. As the facilitator of the seminar, it was my challenge to introduce the nine other learners to the Goffman and Sarason frameworks (see Appendices).

Participants were given time to read the Prologue in the present book, *The Charismatic Leader: The Presentation of Self and the Creation of Educational Settings,* after which discussion ensued. The first question addressed was, "Does this cautionary tale highlighting presentation-of-self difficulties of the junior high school teacher and his principal ring true?" There was unanimous agreement that there is a problem—namely, that some teachers and educational administrators do not present themselves well, and that all teachers and administrators can profit from further attention to this subject. This raised a second question that stimulated discussion in our learning community: "Can educators in preservice and inservice settings have their consciousness raised as to the importance of presentation of self?" Seminar participants answered "Yes" but with some qualifications. They basically said that it is very difficult to reach some educators who have little interest in presentation of self or are afraid to give attention to this matter. Furthermore, all agreed that preservice and advanced teacher and administrator education needs to give more attention to this matter. The discussion took an unexpected turn to problems and prospects with mentoring systems. Seminar members said that it was rare that such systems worked well. Pitfalls in mentoring systems were identified and discussed: too little time to do justice to the mentoring process; subject matter boundaries—particularly at the high school level; and lack of fit between mentor and mentee. One person blurted out, "Some administrators who put a mentoring system in place act as if we can simply push a button and the system will operate effectively. It simply doesn't work this way!" The outspoken educator was apparently sensitive to quick-fix approaches by professional development leaders. Step 1, consciousness raising as to the problem, was obviously achieved as seminar members' comments demonstrated that they now *owned* the problem.

One other reading assignment was made in order to emphasize that the professional development leader brings to this process certain powerful assumptions—sometimes stated and at other times tacit or understood. Seminar participants read the introduction to the present chapter on professional development and a spirited discussion ensued.

Step 2: Introducing the Goffman and Sarason Frameworks. The second step was to provide participants with examples of these frameworks in action by having them read excerpts from the writings of Goffman and Sarason. At the end of the first session, participants agreed to read excerpts from Erving Goffman's (1959) *The Presentation of Self in Everyday Life* and Seymour

Sarason's (1972) *The Creation of Settings* for the next meeting. We spent the first hour of the second session going through these excerpts, but the information didn't have a good deal of meaning until we began applying it in real-life situations. The following checklist was used to assess the presentation-of-self behaviors of prominent speakers whose performances were audio taped or videotaped: Martin Luther King, Jr., Gloria Steinem, Camille Paglia, Reynolds Price, Daniel Levinson, Fred Chappell, Lee Kinard, and William Friday.

THE GOFFMAN FRAMEWORK:
AN OUTLINE TO ASSESS
SPEAKERS' PRESENTATION OF SELF

Key Concept: Assessment of Presenter of Self

Performance: "all of the activity of a given participant on a given occasion which serves to influence in any way any of the other participants" (Goffman, 1959, p. 15).

Authenticity/sincerity: Does the presenter "believe in the impression fostered by his performance" (Goffman, 1959, p. 18)? Convey what he or she claims to be?

Setting: "the scenic parts of expressive equipment" (Lemert & Branaman, 1997, p. 98). Props and other physical features of the stage.

Front: "the expressive equipment of a standard kind intentionally or unwittingly employed by the individual during his performance" (Goffman, 1959, p. 22). For example, titles, clothing, gender, ethnicity, height, looks, posture, patterns of speech, facial expressions, and gestures.

Dramatic realization: Does the presenter mobilize his or her activity "so that it will convey during the interaction what he wishes to convey" (Goffman, 1959, p. 30)?

Idealization: Does the presenter highlight the highest official and stated values of the community and "forgo or conceal action which is inconsistent with these standards" (Goffman, 1959, p. 41)?

Audience segregation: Does the presenter ensure "that those before whom he plays one of his parts will not be the same individuals before whom he plays a different part in another setting" (Goffman, 1959, p. 49)?

Performance risk: Does the presenter "say things that contradict established views of the organization he represents" (Goffman, 1959, p. 63)?

Misrepresentation: Does the presenter "impersonate or pretend to be someone he is not" (Goffman, 1959, p. 70)?

Expressive control: Does the presenter "use his energy and expertise to control the situation" (Goffman, 1959, p. 70)? For example, use a microphone or teleprompter or eye contact, such as "the teacher look."

Mystification: Does the presenter "keep a certain distance from the audience to his advantage" (Goffman, 1959, p. 70)?

Teams and teaming: Does the presenter acknowledge the contributions of others and have his or her ego in check? Is there a "we" quality to the performance (Goffman, 1959)?

Decorum: Does the presenter comport himself well "while in visual or aural range of the audience but not necessarily engaged in talk with them" (Goffman, 1959, p. 107)?

Regional behavior & treatment of the absent: How does the presenter treat those not present (Goffman, 1959)?

The value of this checklist will come alive in the comments of one seminar member's use of the framework: The comments are in response to Martin Luther King's speech at a Michigan Council of Churches meeting at Central Methodist

Church in Detroit on March 15, 1968—a riveting sermon titled "The Meaning of Hope" that was delivered shortly before his death.

This sermon, a powerful *performance*, uses imagery and stories that convey Dr. King's sincerity with regard to social justice. Its *authenticity* is demonstrated by Dr. King's willingness to put all of his resources, including his own life, on the line. The religious *setting*, a large church in Detroit, provided background for Dr. King to convey his message. The *fronts*, such as the titles of "doctor" and "reverend," were used by the minister who introduced him, and Dr. King's patterns of speech were also effectively used to great advantage. For example, there was a cadence in his speech that kept the attention of the *audience*, and the modulation in his voice from relative quiet to a pronounced and lower voice was most effective.

Dramatic realization was achieved as Dr. King drew upon all of his speaking skills to reach his audience. His comments on a moral code that opposed involvement in Vietnam and racism drew upon *idealization*. He also dramatically used *audience segregation* to aim his message at the clergy in the audience.

Dr. King's message was consistent with established views of the organizations he represented, thus not making him a *performance risk*.

He made excellent use of the microphone, a kind of *expressive control* of the *setting*. There was a certain *mystification*, distance from the audience due to his fame and prominence as an international figure.

He also conveyed the belief that he was a leader who needed a team to achieve the goals of the social justice movement. He conveyed a "we" quality regarding work that needed to be done.

Dr. King had excellent *decorum*. He drew upon what seemed to me to be the civilities of the South at the beginning of his speech. He apologized for not being able to stay for a longer period of time at the conference as he had other pressing matters needing his attention. Finally, he made several references in his sermon to those less fortunate who needed everyone's attention. In this way he expressed his concern for *treatment of the absent*.

Step 3: Personalizing the Issues. The third step was the more time-consuming task of having each person write an autobiographical essay using the presentation-of-self theme as an organizing device: "How did I learn presentation-of-self attitudes and skills as an educator?" (See Appendix C for key concepts to consider in writing an autobiographical essay.) We were alert to the connection between substantive issues facing us as educational leaders and the ways we present ourselves in creating educational settings. We returned to the audio and videotapes we had used in order to facilitate our discussions in regard to this connection. The sharing of as much of these essays as each person wished led to a reciprocity of perspectives and identification of commonly held themes. One participant's comments about personalizing the presentation-of-self and creation of educational settings theme is a powerful reminder of this process: "I started teaching in an urban school with high-risk students and then moved to a suburban school whose parents presented us with a very different set of problems. I have been an assistant principal at a Title I school for the last three years and find that this is where I want to be." She added, "As a result of writing my autobiography, I've decided to do a doctoral dissertation on social justice. I want to take courses and have experiences during the remainder of my doctoral study that will prepare me to do this. Doing autobiography taught me a good deal about myself but it also opened me up to a world that is less than perfect—a leadership challenge."

The autobiographical essays demonstrated the powerful influence of significant others and their ways of presenting themselves: parents, siblings, extended family members, teachers, coaches, and friends.

Step 4: Creating Professional Development Plans. Prior to our developing professional development plans, we read and discussed Chapter 1, "The Civilities of Leadership: Attitudes, Behaviors, Tools, and Skills" and Chapter 2, "Teams, Teaming, and the Creation of Educational Settings." These chapters provided seminar participants with concrete information on the presentation of

Figure 3.1   "Elements of a Professional Development Plan . . ."

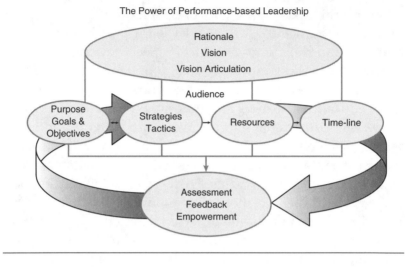

self and the creation of educational settings. With background knowledge from all of our work together to this point, we moved to the next challenge—the construction of a professional development model that would be a graphic depiction or map for the creation of a professional development plan (PDP) for an educational setting of each person's choice.

Figure 3.1, "Elements of a Professional Development Plan for Improving the Presentation of Self and the Creation of Educational Settings: The Power of Performance-based Leadership," illustrates the necessary components in our framework or model. *Rationale* refers to the fundamental reasons or assumptions underlying other components. Rationale becomes the basis for *vision* and its clear *articulation*. The research of Bruce Joyce clearly demonstrates the importance of a well-formulated and articulated rationale (Sparks, 1998). Rationale consists of a reasoned statement of guiding principles—the basic assumptions held by professional development leaders. *Purpose* is the overall reason for doing something, *goals* are general statements of intent, and *objectives* are specific statements of intent, usually stated in behaviorally observable terms. Purpose, goals, and objectives are *educational* ends that give participants a common understanding of expectations. Educational ends are useful as they convey to educators and audiences outside of schools and school systems that leaders know what they are doing and are willing to be accountable for reaching well-defined benchmarks. Educational ends can also be motivating to leaders and those they influence.

The central location of *audience* in Figure 3.1 demonstrates its importance. Audience simply refers to those who attend to others' performances. We are reminded that Goffman uses the term performance to mean "all the activity of a given participant on a given occasion which serves to influence in any way any of the other participants" (Goffman, 1959, p. 15). The nature and size of the audience must be considered by the person giving a performance.

Strategies are usually large-scale, long-range activities for achieving goals whereas *tactics* are smaller, short-range maneuvers designed to meet objectives. Tactics tend to have a zigzag nature. *Resources,* human and nonhuman, are essential means of support. A *time-line* is a linear representation of what will be done and when. It is essential for planning, implementation, and follow-up. *Assessment* is the evaluation of worth of the various elements within the model. *Feedback* from all parties is essential so that modifications can be made if needed. Those involved in assessment must be mindful that some things will need to be conserved while other things will need to be changed. Effective performance-based leadership encourages the *empowerment* of participants. Those who are empowered have the feeling of ownership of an idea or program.

Of the ten North Carolina educators who participated in the seminar activities, three are in higher education and seven are in K–12 schools. One is a principal in an alternative school, Grades 4–12, one is an assistant principal in an elementary school, two are assistant principals in middle schools, three are assistant principals in high schools, and one is a teacher in a high school.

After brainstorming possible topics, each of the educators chose a topic for which he or she had a passion. Two of the educators in higher education focused on preservice teacher education, with the third person giving attention to instructors in a community college. Educators in K–12 settings chose the following topics: classroom management, parent-teacher communication, substitute teachers, initially licensed teachers, teachers, and administrators.

As we created our professional development plans, a number of commonly held challenges emerged. How can people in the target audience who are insensitive to their presentation-of-self problems become enlightened without our backing them into a corner so that they become defensive obstructionists? How can required attendance for professional development activities be "enforced" without eroding morale? How can our enthusiasm for professional development activities on the presentation-of-self theme be conveyed to participants in an effective way? How can we as professional development leaders empower those being led? What can participants be expected to read as part of professional development activities? These questions surfaced as seminar members presented their plans to others in the learning community. It fact, it was this sharing of plans that was most helpful to participants in sharpening their ideas and writing. It moved participants from the role of reactor to actor, and it took some time before presenters became comfortable in their new role. Those seminar members who reacted to presenters improved their ability to critique—something we defined as review, adoption of a thesis (big idea), and support for this thesis. It was suggested that participants in any learning community could improve their ability to critique by being members of book and article reading clubs. This would give members of such clubs the opportunity to practice talking to each other about important ideas—good practice indeed in anticipation of talking to parents and other adults interested in schools.

As we considered the importance of implementing professional development plans, Sarason's ideas on educational change began to come into play with increasing frequency.

We returned to Sarason's ideas, discussed previously. Members of our learning community used their experience in schools and universities to warn each other about what could go wrong when putting professional development ideas into action. Special concern was expressed during our discussions for relating to members of our settings who would openly oppose or simply not seriously consider our ideas. We also reminded ourselves that in order for some things to change, other things would have to be conserved. One seminar participant summarized the feelings of the entire learning community with what she considered the most important contribution Sarason made to her thinking:

> Sarason taught me that the culture of the school must be the focus of my educational leadership. Presentation of self is more than a technical matter. It always takes place within a context. Professional development experiences of a stop-gap nature will only reinforce faddism.

In short, the powerful ideas expressed by Sarason in his writings had new meaning for seminar participants on the firing line.

On several occasions during our 15 weeks together, participants discussed problems and prospects associated with videotaping teachers and administrators as part of preservice and advanced education experiences. We recognized the powerful impact this tool could have in giving teachers and administrators feedback on their presentation of self. We knew that it would take time for participants to become comfortable with this experience and we agreed that the sharing of videotapes with others should be voluntary.

Step Number 5: The Implementation of Professional Development Plans. The fifth step followed the 15-week seminar. A communication network was in place as a result of the seminar so that members of the learning community could share ideas and give each other emotional support.

CONCLUSION

We learned several important things from our 15-week seminar. First, there is no substitute for positive energy within the learning community. Our wanting to be with each other and our passion for the topic at hand served as the fuel for this positive energy. Second, there had to be enough structure to give us a sense of security and direction but not so much that it inhibited our creativity. The facilitator provided an agenda for each session and a summary of progress from the previous meeting. Seminar members were invited to suggest ways in which the agendas and summaries could be improved. The concreteness of creating professional development plans gave us confidence, according to one participant. She added, "We experienced success by making our expectations clear in the plans." Third, pressure to attend sessions and do good work—speaking, reading, and writing—came from the learning community itself. Participants didn't want to let others in the community down by not doing good work. Preparation for each meeting was simply expected. There was no hiding like there is in many learning situations. Fourth, we operated for the most part in the middle ground between theory and practice—ground where theory informed practice and practice informed theory. Participants' ownership really "kicked in" at the point where professional development plans needed to be created. One person remarked, "Each plan, like our professional autobiographies, is so personal and unique." Fifth, we reached out to use as many human and nonhuman resources as we could, given the topic we had identified. Guest speakers, in class and on campus, gave us access to substantive content and provided us with examples of presentation of self. The Internet and library were important sources of research sources. Books, articles, audio- and video tapes, and the like brought life to our seminar. In the process we were introduced to a number of research and writing tools. Doing autobiography helped us understand the value of narrative research. The best Web site we found on presentation of self, www.amme.com, has free articles by Richard ("Rick") Amme, media coach and crisis management consultant.

It was very interesting to see how the talents of participants emerged as the learning community evolved. For example, Jean Camp, whose expertise in computer science and program development became obvious, emerged as the natural person to go to the board and sketch the first draft of our professional development model. Brian Toth, an assistant high school principal with excellent computer skills became our bibliographer. A visit by President George W. Bush to John Slade's community college prompted an excellent discussion of presentation-of-self skills and the politics of leadership. Bonnie Roane, an assistant high school principal who had served in the United States Army, drew upon her experience to explain how presentation of self was emphasized in the armed forces. Mary James, an administrator in an Eckerd Youth Alternatives Camp, helped us see how visits to other Eckerd camps inspired her to create a professional development plan that would improve presentation of self in her own work setting. Joy Gomez, Quanda Turner, and Nancy Moody used their experience in other states to check any provincial tendencies we had, and Tyrone Gold and Jason Johnson helped us see how important presentation-of-self activities are in middle school settings. It was in the sharing of our talents with each other that we became a true learning community.

SUGGESTED READINGS

Darling-Hammond, L., & McLaughlin, M. W. (1995). Policies that support professional development in an era of reform. *Phi Delta Kappan, 76,* 597–604.

Darling-Hammond, L. (1997). *The right to learn: A blueprint for creating schools that work.* San Francisco: Jossey-Bass.

Diaz-Maggioli, G. (2004). *Teacher-centered professional development.* Alexandria, VA: Association for Supervision & Curriculum Development.

Fullan, M. (2001). *Leading in a culture of change.* San Francisco: Jossey-Bass.

Gordon, S. P. (2004). *Professional development for school improvement: Empowering learning communities.* Boston: Pearson.

Hall, G. E., & Hord, S. M. (1987). *Change in schools: Facilitating the process.* Albany: State of New York University Press.

Hall, G. E., & Hord, S. M. (2001). *Implementing change: Patterns, principles, and potholes.* Boston: Allyn & Bacon.

Joyce, B. (1990). *Changing school culture through staff development.* Alexandria, VA: Association for Supervision & Curriculum Development.

Sparks, D. (2004). *Leading for results: Transforming teaching, learning and relationships in schools.* Thousand Oaks, CA: Corwin Press.

Appendix A

*An Outline for Professional
Development Leaders Who Use
This Book to Help Teachers
and Administrators Improve
Their Presentation of Self*

1. *Introduction.* The following guidelines should be helpful as you use ideas from this book to introduce teachers and/or administrators in professional development settings to the presentation-of-self theme. The guidelines emerged from a pilot program I describe in Chapter 3. References to parts of the present book will be made in the following outline. You, the reader and professional development leader, are urged to use the header quotes at the beginning of each chapter to stimulate discussion.

2. *Preparing the Way.* As the professional development leader, it is wise for you to be clear as to different ways in which *professional development* is defined. Chapter 3 begins with a discussion of definitions of professional development. In the event that you have colleagues who will help you lead professional development activities on the presentation of self, it would be good for all of you to read and discuss this section of Chapter 3. This is also true of the second section of Chapter 3 on basic assumptions underlying professional development. At some time during the course of your professional development

activities on the presentation of self, you may wish to discuss your ideas on professional development with participants. It may be helpful to outline the main ideas from the first two sections of Chapter 3 in order to share them with participants. Please keep in mind that these ideas are a *springboard* that invites educators to add their views of what professional development *has been, is,* and *should be.* Figure 3.1, "Elements of a Professional Development Plan for Improving the Presentation of Self and the Creation of Educational Settings," is in Chapter 3. It may be a kind of graphic road map for your professional development leadership.

3. *Consciousness Raising.* Participants will need a few minutes to read the Prologue, "A Cautionary Tale." You may then ask the question, "Does this cautionary tale highlighting presentation-of-self difficulties of a junior high teacher and his principal ring true?" You may also ask, "Is it really the case that some teachers and administrators do not present themselves well and can profit from further professional development on this matter?" (You may wish to ask participants to react to your assumption that the educators as professionals should be able to articulate what they are doing and why.) Next, you may brainstorm with participants as to ways in which this professional development challenge can and should be addressed. Finally, it will be helpful to find out if participants have had the presentation-of-self issue addressed in their preservice or advanced education experiences. Their responses will provide you, the professional development leader, with baseline information that you can build on as professional development experiences take place.

4. *Introducing the Goffman Framework.* Chapter 3 describes the presentation-of-self framework constructed by Erving Goffman. You may wish to highlight their ideas before assigning this reading to participants. We found that the Goffman framework checklist in Chapter 3, when applied to videotapes of prominent speakers, brought life to the frameworks and taught participants to use presentation-of-self concepts. Audiotapes may also be used.

5. *Personalizing the Issues.* Now that participants have applied presentation-of-self concepts to others viewed on videotapes, they should be able to use these concepts to assess their own presentation of self. You may wish to be videotaped yourself in a variety of situations, after which you can share the results with educators you are leading. You and participants may use the Goffman checklist in Chapter 3 to analyze your presentation of self. This self-revelation will serve as a powerful example for participants. It will demonstrate your willingness to learn from your presentation-of-self activities and show the kind of courage that it takes to assess your own strengths and weaknesses. The next step is for participants to participate in this exercise, after which they can voluntarily share the results with others of their own choosing.

Another approach to personalizing issues related to presentation of self is to focus on the question, "How did I learn presentation-of-self attitudes and skills?" A related question is, "Who were the significant persons in my life who taught me these attitudes and skills?" Participants may do autobiography on this theme by verbally sharing their stories and also do some writing of essays if you, the professional development leader, and they wish to explore this outlet.

You may expand the personalizing of presentation-of-self issues by having participants read Chapters 1 and 2. Chapter 1, "The Civilities of Leadership: Attitudes, Behaviors, Tools, and Skills," argues that speaking, listening, and writing always take place within a context, such as the culture of a school, and this culture has a personality in the same way that a person has a personality. Chapter 2, "Teams, Teaming, and the Creation of Educational Settings," demonstrates how creative educational leaders use their talents to help others identify and use their talents—a process that depends on teams and teaming. Learning communities result from participation in these creative activities.

6. *Conclusion.* The guidelines above are simply a springboard designed to help you, the professional development leader, use your creative abilities in dealing with the presentation of self and the creation of educational settings. Those

who participated in our pilot program (described in Chapter 3) created their own, highly personal professional development plans—something that all of us in this learning community celebrated. We wish you well as you use your positive energies to deal with this important subject.

Appendix B

What Works and Doesn't Work in Doing Professional Development?

You may do this exercise alone or in a small group. If you are in a small group setting, name (a) a facilitator and (b) a note taker or reporter.

Please *identify* and *place in priority order* three things you've discovered do work well in doing professional development and three things that don't work well in doing professional development. (Priority order refers to strength of response.)

Three Things That Work Well in Doing Professional Development	Three Things That Don't Work Well in Doing Professional Development
1.	1.
2.	2.
3.	3.

If you have met in a small group, have each group's note taker or reporter summarize findings from small group deliberations.

_____

_____

_____

_____

_____

Appendix C

Concepts to Consider in
Doing Your Autobiography on
the Theme, "How I Learned to
Present Myself and Give Leadership
to the Creation of Educational Settings"

When participants in our pilot program on the presentation of self and the creation of educational settings did their autobiographies, we discovered the following organizing concepts were shared by this community of learners (see Chapter 3). I have included some examples from participants' autobiographies to illustrate the concepts.

1. *Sense of place:* Seminar members mentioned matters that influenced their senses: a description of the sky at different seasons of the year, weather patterns in the various seasons of the year, geography (mountains, hills, trees, flatlands, lakes, oceans, etc.), urban, suburban, and rural settings, and highways. How do you describe your sense of place?

_____

_____

2. *Sense of time:* Participants in our pilot program said that this varied according to the place they lived during different times in their lives—urban, suburban, and rural. They also said

that their view of time changed during the different seasons of their lives. How do you describe your sense of time?

_____

_____

3. *Family influences:* Parents, siblings, and relatives played a part in how seminar members learned to present themselves and create educational settings. How did various family members, immediate and extended, influence your presentation of self and leadership in creating educational settings?

_____

_____

4. *The influence of friends and mentors:* This influence varied a good deal from one participant to another. Some seminar members seemed to "go it alone," whereas others were highly influenced by friends and mentors. Did friends and mentors influence your presentation of self and leadership in creating educational settings, and if so, how?

_____

_____

5. *The influence of education—formal and informal:* Schools, colleges, and universities influenced most seminar participants in both their formal education and informal learning. How did these institutions influence your presentation of self and leadership in creating educational settings?

_____

_____

6. *Vocational and world influences were important influences:* Seminar members especially cited how their first real jobs set the norms for their vocational growth and development. How did these influences affect you?

_____

_____

7. *Religious influences were cited by most seminar members:* In some cases, formal religions played a major role in shaping persons' presentation of self and leadership in creating educational settings—in both positive and negative ways. Other persons chose to talk about spiritual matters.

Please describe how these issues influenced your presentation of self and leadership in creating educational settings.

_____

_____

8. *Power of "the dream" as an influence on presentation of self and leadership in creating educational settings:* Many seminar members referred to their dream as an important influence on their leadership and presentation of self. In some cases, this dream of what they could become as adults took root in childhood; in other situations, this dream developed during their experience in higher education. If this was an influence on you, please describe this influence on your presentation of self and leadership in creating educational settings.

_____

_____

9. *Power of your "worldview" as an influence on your leadership and presentation of self:* Some of the members of the seminar had a strong philosophy or view of what the world should and can be. A combination of the forces described above came to play in the formation of this worldview. Does this concept have meaning for you, and if so, how has your worldview influenced your presentation of self and leadership in creating educational settings?

_____

_____

Appendix D

A Presentation-of-Self Change and Conservation Inventory

N ow that you have background knowledge concerning the presentation of self and the creation of educational settings, please answer the following inventory items:

My Name _____

What are five things about my presentation of self that I highly value and want to conserve?

1. _____

2. _____

3. _____

4. _____

5. _____

What are five things about my presentation of self that I want to change—five challenges I will work on to improve my presentation of self?

1. _____

2. _____

3. _____

4. _____

5. _____

Appendix E

Belief in Oneself and the Presentation of Self

P at Conroy (2002), well-known author, looks back on his experience as a basketball player at The Citadel in amazement and shares with us his view that

> belief in oneself—authentic, inviolable, and unshakable belief, not the undercutting kind—is necessary to all human achievement. Once I began believing in myself and not listening to the people who did not believe in me, I turned myself into a point guard who you needed to watch. (p. 398)

Please list the people and their actions that helped you achieve this authentic belief in self.

1. _____

2. _____

3. _____

4. _____

5. _____

Please list the people and their actions that worked against your achieving authentic belief in self.

1. _____

2. _____

3. _____

4. _____

5. _____

Finally, please list any advice you can give to others in order to help them achieve authentic belief in self. In other words, what lessons learned can you share with them on this matter?

1. _____

2. _____

3. _____

4. _____

5. _____

Appendix F

Turning Breakdowns (Losses) Into Breakthroughs (Victories)

Pat Conroy (2002), author of *My Losing Season*, the story of his senior year on The Citadel's basketball team, gives us sound advice on what we can learn from losses as we engage in presentation-of-self activities: "Losing prepares you for the heartbreak, setback, and tragedy that you will encounter in the world more than winning ever can. By licking your wounds you learn how to avoid getting wounded the next time." He adds that he believes this "because you have to face things clearly and you cannot turn away from what is true" (p. 395).

Please list some of the losses you have experienced in presentation-of-self activities. Follow each loss you have identified with the lesson you learned from this experience.

Loss

Lesson Learned

_____ _____

_____ _____

_____ _____

_____ _____

_____ _____

Appendix G

The Impostor Complex and the Presentation of Self

Arthur M. Schlesinger, Jr. (2000), renowned Harvard historian and special assistant to President John F. Kennedy, writes:

> Although I now rather enjoyed lecturing, I never quite escaped the impostor complex, the fear that I would one day be found out. My knowledge was by some standards considerable, but it was outweighed by my awareness of my ignorance. I always saw myself skating over thin ice. The impostor complex had its value. It created a great reluctance, for example, to impose my views on students. (p. 439)

Goffman (1959) recognized this same phenomenon in performers who thought, no matter how well their performances went, that they were using "tricks" to win over the audience.

Please use the following space to describe those times in your presentation of self when you experienced the impostor complex:

_____

_____

Appendix H

Conflict, Freedom, Change, Discovery, and the Presentation of Self

Arthur M. Schlesinger, Jr. (2000) believes that conflict, freedom, change, and discovery are essential ingredients in a democracy:

> So long as society stays free, so long will it continue in a state of tension, breeding contradiction, breeding strife. But, conflict is also the guarantee of freedom; it is the instrument of change; it is above all, the source of discovery, the source of art, the source of love. (pp. 521–522)

Please describe the experiences you have had when conflict has been the instrument of change as well as the source of discovery, art, and love. Finally, share how these experiences have informed and influenced your presentation of self.

_____

_____

_____

_____

_____

Appendix I

Entrance and Exit Rituals

E ntrance and exit rituals provide the educational leader with an excellent opportunity to use presentation-of-self skills (see Chapter 1). This inventory is designed for you to write notes about entrance and exit rituals that *do exist* and *should exist* in the setting in which you are a leader.

What <u>entrance</u> rituals presently exist in the setting in which you are a leader?	What <u>entrance</u> rituals should exist in the setting in which you are a leader?
1.	1.
2.	2.
3.	3.

What <u>exit</u> rituals presently exist in the setting in which you are a leader?	What <u>exit</u> rituals should exist in the setting in which you are a leader?
1.	1.
2.	2.
3.	3.

Appendix J

The Presentation of Self and the Power of Critique

C ritique is essential to any educator interested in the presentation of self and the creation of educational settings. It is sometimes defined as the art or practice of criticism. However, critique can be much more than this deficit definition that focuses on what is wrong or missing. Critique occurs when the leader (a) reviews what has taken place, (b) adopts a point of view (thesis) as to what took place, and (c) supports this point of view or thesis. Please give examples of your engagement in critique during a typical workday:

1. _____

2. _____

3. _____

What are some of the subtle dynamics involved in bringing excellence to critique? The first is *discernment*. To discern is to see clearly or differentiate the important from the less important. Making such a judgment always depends on a particular *context*. In other words, one must move beyond generalizations to describe clearly what is happening within a context. For example, Paul is a seventh grader who is called to the principal's office for possessing metallic knuckles. The principal knows that metallic knuckles are considered a weapon—an offense that carries a ten-day, out-of-school suspension. The principal is aware that this is a first offense for Paul, as well as the fact that Paul is living with his grandmother because his father is in jail and Paul's alcoholic mother is living with a man who is a drug addict. In fact, Paul got the metallic knuckles from this man. The principal, the school resource officer, Paul, and Paul's grandmother had a lengthy discussion during which Paul was visibly shaken by the gravity of what he had done. The principal's presentation of self demonstrated his serious attitude toward the situation while at the same time the principal was sensitive to the context of Paul's home life and the role that the school context could play in relating to Paul. The principal, on consultation with the school resource officer, decided to give Paul a three-day, in-school suspension with the understanding that a second offense would automatically kick in a ten-day, out-of-school suspension.

Please briefly describe one or more situations in which you used discernment within a particular context to reach what you considered to be a fair and reasonable decision.

_____

_____

_____

_____

_____

Appendix K

Focusing on the Message
Relieves Nervousness

R ichard ("Rick") Amme (2003b) recommends the following
exercise to demonstrate that your connection as a speaker
to the message you have a passion for can alleviate nervousness.

He asks each person in a small group of seminar participants to focus on an emotional event in her or his life. Each
person is expected to talk about this event without rehearsal
or notes. The event may be joyful or sad. Each participant has
five to ten minutes to tell the group about this event.

Rick has found that participants are often somewhat stiff
at the beginning of this impromptu presentation, but they
quickly become less self-conscious and begin to gesture and
have more inflection in their voices.

It is important in the discussion that follows this exercise
to note that speakers often are not conscious of the emerging
changes in their presentations. It is also worth noting how
transfixed listeners become as they listen to the presenters. *The
most significant finding, however, is that the content of the messages
moved presenters beyond their concern for presentation-of-self tech-
nique.* Rick reminds members of the group that their gift to
speak well is already within each person.

Appendix L

The "Table Manners" of
Student Leadership in Higher Education

Going to college can be among the more enjoyable and rewarding experiences students can have. Students are introduced to new theories, concepts, and practices. An opportunity to reflect on and integrate learning in relation to previous experiences is afforded. Students encounter many persons with varying backgrounds, talents, interests, and aspirations—the substance of personal growth. A value of higher education study is the opportunity to demonstrate maturity and self-direction. Professors are a vehicle to assist in this growth and development. The following guidelines are designed to facilitate clear student–professor communication and enhance presentation-of-self skills and attitudes.

A. Basic Assumptions Faculty Often Bring to This Process:

1. Students should play a proactive role, not simply a reactive one.

2. As part of program planning, students should have and be familiar with the college or university catalogue.

3. Students should demonstrate maturity by recognizing the importance of "due dates" and meeting them.

4. If a substantive reaction to student writing is called for on the part of a professor, students should negotiate this well in advance.

5. When a student submits a written document to a professor, clean copy is required. Use a good copy editor or proofreader to ensure this.

6. Open communication, rather than "hidden agendas," is the key to mutual respect and consideration.

7. The scholarly responsibility a student assumes in pre-paration for and in reacting to class is as important as responsibility assumed in class.

8. Effective oral and written communication is a key to successful student leadership in college and beyond.

9. Removing and minimizing "irritants" lead to a better relationship with professors.

10. As part of the negotiation process, students and pro-fessors should clearly state their expectations. (Note: Most professors have a nine-month contract. Some teach during the summer. Few are available for all 12 months of the year.)

B. If you want satisfaction as a student,

1. Ask the professor's secretary for the professor's office hours and call during this time. Also ask for the pro-fessor's e-mail address if this is not in the course syllabus distributed during the first class period.

2. With regard to telephone calls to campus, if the professor isn't in, leave your name, telephone number, the nature of your business, and the best time to return the call.

3. For efficient and effective use of time, prepare for the content of the telephone conversation.

4. Identify yourself at the onset of the conversation on the phone.

5. When substantive agreements are arrived at over the telephone, the student should follow up with an e-mail

or memorandum of understanding concluding with "Unless I hear from you otherwise, I'll assume this is correct."

6. Don't have secretaries, in the event that you have one, place calls to faculty members that put faculty on hold until the caller is available to talk.

7. Remember to copy appropriate parties via e-mail or memoranda.

8. In some cases, give a self-addressed, stamped envelope to the professor for a sure response.

9. Log important contacts with professors with date, time, and outline of content in your log.

10. Clearly state what you expect of the professor when corresponding with him or her.

11. It is probably wise in most cases to use a fairly formal style when e-mailing a professor.

Appendix M

What Characterizes the Teacher
Who Presents Self Well During Open
House/Walk-the-Schedule Night at School?

Consensus was reached by seminar participants, teachers, and administrators on the following characteristics. Seminar participants had just participated in a discussion of the Prologue to the present book:

1. Physical appearance conveys professionalism. Dresses and grooms well.

2. Uses good English.

3. Is prepared for the event. Well organized. Any materials distributed are clearly written and have been proofread for errors. (These behaviors demonstrate that the teacher values this evening's events—wants to be at the event.)

4. Knows parent's child and is interested in his or her progress. Has something positive to say about the child.

5. Conveys a passion for teaching—wants to be a teacher.

6. Is self-assured without being arrogant. Conveys ability to manage students and create a safe classroom.

7. Demonstrates knowledge of the subject and how to teach it. Leaves the parent with the feeling that his or her child will be involved in meaningful activity.

8. Understands and can articulate the relationship between what he or she teaches and what other teachers teach.

9. Has created an inviting physical setting in the classroom.

10. Has and can articulate a vision for teaching and learning. Can articulate what has been done, is being done, and will be done and the rationale for this.

References

Adams, J. G. (1983). *Without precedent*. New York: Horton.

Amme, R. (2003a). The lost art of listening. *Media Crisis Management*, pp. 1-5. Retrieved from www.amme.com

Amme, R. (2003b). Presentations and speeches. "It's not the voice, it's the message!" *Media Crisis Management*, pp. 1–5. Retrieved from www.amme.com

Amme, R. (2003c). When communicating—to thine own self be true. *Media Crisis Management*, pp. 1–4. Retrieved from www.amme.com

Austin, G., & Brubaker, D. L. (1988). Making the right calls. *Piedmont Airlines, 15,* 103–105.

Brubaker, D. L. (1982). *Curriculum planning: The dynamics of theory and practice.* Glenview, IL: Scott, Foresman.

Brubaker, D. L. (2004). *Creative curriculum leadership: Inspiring and empowering your school community* (2nd ed.). Thousand Oaks, CA: Corwin Press.

Brubaker, D. L., & Coble, L. D. (1997). *Staying on track: An educational leader's guide to preventing derailment and ensuring personal and organizational success.* Thousand Oaks, CA: Corwin Press.

Brubaker, D. L., & Coble, L. D. (2005). *The hidden leader: Leadership lessons on the potential within.* Thousand Oaks, CA: Corwin Press.

Brubaker, D. L., & Nelson, R. (1974). *Creative survival in educational bureaucracies.* Berkeley, CA: McCutchan.

Buckley, W. (1982). *Atlantic high.* Boston: Little, Brown.

Burns, D. D. (1980). *Feeling good.* New York: Signet.

Califano, J. A., Jr. (2004). *Inside: A public and private life.* New York: Public Affairs.

Collins, D. (2000). *Achieving your vision of professional development: How to assess your needs and get what you want.* Greensboro, NC: SERVE.

Conroy, P. (2002). *My losing season.* New York: Doubleday.

Cranston, N. (2000). Teachers as leaders: A critical agenda for the new millennium. *Asia-Pacific Journal of Teacher Education, 28,* 123–132.

Darling-Hammond, L. (1997). *The right to learn: A blueprint for creating schools that work.* San Francisco: Jossey-Bass.

Dixon, N. (1995). *A practical model for organizational learning.* Greensboro, NC: Center for Creative Leadership Issues and Observations.

Epstein, J. L. (2001). *School, family, and community partnership.* Boulder, CO: Westview.

Fried, R. (1996). *The passionate teacher: How teachers and parents can help children reclaim the joy of discovery.* Boston: Beacon.

Fried, R. (2001). *The passionate learner: A practical guide* (2nd ed.). Boston: Beacon.

Fullan, M. (2001). *Leading in a culture of change.* San Francisco: Jossey-Bass.

Goffman, E. (1959). *The presentation of self in everyday life.* New York: Doubleday Anchor.

Goffman, E. (1967). *Interaction ritual: Essays on face-to-face behavior.* New York: Doubleday, Anchor.

Gordon, S. P. (2004). *Professional development for school improvement: Empowering learning communities.* Boston: Pearson.

King, M. L., Jr. (1968, March 15). *The meaning of hope.* Sermon given to clergy at Central Methodist Church, Detroit, Michigan.

Kleinfield, S. (1989). *The hotel.* New York: Simon & Schuster.

Lemert, C., & Branaman, A. (Eds.). (1997). *The Goffman reader.* Oxford, UK: Blackwell.

Lieberman, A., & Miller, L. (1999). *Teachers transforming their world and their work.* New York: Teachers College Press.

Linver, S. (1978). *Speakeasy.* New York: Summit.

Peck, M. S. (1978). *The road less traveled.* New York: Simon & Schuster.

Peck, M. S. (1987). *The different drum.* New York: Simon & Schuster.

Peck, M. S. (1993). *A world awaiting to be born: Civility rediscovered.* New York: Bantam.

Raywid, M. (1993). Finding time for collaboration. *Educational Leadership, 50*(1), 30–35.

Reich, R. B. (1997). *Locked in the cabinet.* New York: Knopf.

Russell, W., & Branch, T. (1979). *Second wind: Memoirs of an opinionated man.* New York: Random House.

Sarason, S. B. (1972). *The creation of settings and the future societies.* San Francisco: Jossey-Bass.

Sarason, S. B. (1996). *Revisiting the culture of the school and the problem of change.* New York: Teachers College Press.

Sarason, S. B. (1999). *Teaching as a performing art.* New York: Teachers College Press.

Sarason, S. B. (2002). *Educational reform: A self scrutinizing memoir.* New York: Teachers College Press.

Sarason, S. B. (2004). *And what do you mean by learning?* Portsmouth, NH: Heinemann.

Schieffer, B. (2003). *This just in: What I couldn't tell you on TV.* New York: Putnam.

Schlesinger, A. M., Jr. (2000). *A life in the twentieth century: Innocent beginnings, 1917–1950.* Boston: Houghton Mifflin.

Shcharansky, A. (1986, February 24). Visit with a survivor. *Time*, p. 38.

Senge, P. M. (1990). *The fifth discipline: The art & practice of the learning organization.* New York: Currency Doubleday.

Smith, H. (1988). *The power game.* New York: Random House.

Sparks, D. (1998, Fall). Interview with Bruce Joyce: Making assessment part of teacher learning. *Journal of Staff Development, 19*(4), 1–4.

Tell, C. (2001, February). Appreciating good teaching. *Educational Leadership, 58,* 6–11.

Time. (1993, January 4). p. 55.

Woodward, B. (1999). *Shadow: Five presidents and the legacy of Watergate.* New York: Simon & Schuster.

Zahorik, J., & Brubaker, D. (1972). *Toward more humanistic instruction.* Dubuque, IA: William C. Brown.

Index

**CORWIN
PRESS**

The Corwin Press logo—a raven striding across an open book—
represents the union of courage and learning. Corwin Press is
committed to improving education for all learners by publishing
books and other professional development resources for those
serving the field of PreK–12 education. By providing practical, hands-
on materials, Corwin Press continues to carry out the promise of its
motto: **"Helping Educators Do Their Work Better."**